# THE REMARKABLE LIFE OF
# JAMES BEECHER

*The Beaverkill: The History of a River and its People*

*Trout Fishing in the Catskills*

*The Beaverkill: The History of a River and its People,*
*Expanded and Revised 2ⁿᵈ Edition*

# THE REMARKABLE LIFE OF
# JAMES BEECHER

*Ed Van Put*

ED VAN PUT

BEAVERKILL BOOKS

LIVINGSTON MANOR, NEW YORK

Published in the United States by Beaverkill Books, LLC

Livingston Manor, New York

www.beaverkillbooks.com

Printed in the United States of America

First hardcover edition June 19, 2021

*Book designed by Lee Van Put*

Library of Congress Cataloging-in-Publication Data has been applied for.

LCCN 2021909587

ISBN 978-1-7372371-0-5

10 9 8 7 6 5 4 3 2 1

*Dedicated to those who help the needy.*

# Contents

Mill Brook Ridge

Balsam
Lake
Mountain

Beecher
Lake

Balsam Lake

Tunis
Pond

Beaver Kill

Sand Pond

# Introduction

I first learned about James Chaplin Beecher in the mid-1990s while researching for the book *The Beaverkill: The History of a River and its People*. James Beecher was among the early fly fishermen who fished the Beaverkill at a time when the river contained only one species of trout—the native brook trout. Research involved using Interlibrary Loan and visiting many libraries, including the New York State Library in Albany and the New York Public Library in New York City, and viewing microfilm of newspapers and periodicals.

I began to acquire information about James Beecher and the life he led before he lived in the Beaverkill Valley, including his distinguished career in the Union Army during the Civil War. Early reports indicated Beecher was considered a "free spirit" and a non-conformist. He was also the youngest member of the famous Beecher family of abolitionists, alongside prominent siblings including Henry Ward Beecher, the nation's most influential preacher, and Harriet Beecher Stowe, author of "Uncle Tom's Cabin." His love of nature and his surroundings, as well as his qualities of kindness, compassion, and self-sacrifice, heightened my desire to learn more about him.

My research at the time was limited; it was not until after I acquired a computer that I was able to search more thoroughly. Surprisingly little had been written about James Beecher, despite his incredible experiences. Using a range of historical sources including Beecher's personal correspondence, this work portrays the moving story of a man who selflessly devoted his life to the liberation and betterment of others during a tumultuous time in U.S. history, with his equally determined, extraordinary wife at his side.

From early ordeals in China to his astoundingly courageous service in the Civil War, James Beecher sacrificed a life of privilege to serve as sailor, missionary, preacher, and humanitarian. After signing on as Chaplain in the Union Army during the Civil War, Beecher quickly became Captain of a rifle company to better serve his country leading men into battle. He was later appointed Colonel of the 1st North Carolina Colored Volunteers, an all-black regiment comprised of men who were former slaves, and earned a reputation as a believer in equality. He fought for his men to have the same rights and privileges as other soldiers, to receive equal pay and equal benefits.

Beecher survived the war, ending his military career as a General while helping to rebuild a war-torn nation, but he struggled to cope with his experiences on the front lines for the rest of his life. The book follows Beecher from his initial work as a preacher overseas through unimaginable horrors in the Civil War, post-war turmoil, and the spiritual salvation he found after the war as an early pioneer in the wilds of the Beaverkill Valley. James and his wife Frances (whom he affectionately called Frankie) settled in that lightly inhabited, densely forested area in 1875, and quickly became cherished members of their community, aiding their neighbors through their kindness, generosity, and benevolence.

Described within are the hardships and joys of a simple but fulfilling life deep in the forest. Despite their love of the region, the Beechers' time in this pastoral paradise came to an end; the pull of the pulpit and the weight of expectations James faced as a Beecher led to a life-long struggle between service and seeking sanctuary.

The text offers a thoroughly researched, intimate look at an inspiring man who lived a remarkable life and followed his convictions of equality, kindness, and dedication. 19th Century artwork and photographs are used throughout the book to give a sense of time and place, along with recent color photography of Beecher Lake. Following the text, a selection of James Beecher's personal correspondence is presented in both facsimile and transcription, including letters composed on battlefields and in hospitals, printed for their insight to the urgency and emotion that is visible in the hand-written pages.

This book was written to raise awareness of a kind and honorable man, who was devoted to helping the needy and less fortunate, readily risking his life for freedom and equality for all.

# THE REMARKABLE LIFE OF
# JAMES BEECHER

# 1

## The Headwaters of the Beaverkill
and John Burroughs

There is a small trout lake located in the Catskill Mountains at the headwaters of the Beaverkill River known as Beecher Lake. The lake was named by James Beecher, a remarkable man who led an extraordinary life of journey, adventure, and compassion.

Beecher Lake is one of three lakes that lie at the headwaters, in a lightly inhabited, densely forested area defined by a series of peaks known as the Mill Brook Ridge. Elevations are more than 2,800 feet, with Balsam Lake Mountain being among the highest in the Catskills at 3,720 feet. Just easterly of Balsam Lake Mountain lies Graham Mountain, which is slightly higher at 3,868 feet, and between Graham and Doubletop Mountain lies the source of the Beaverkill.

The headwaters of the river are found deep in the forest, far from any road, in a narrow, rocky ravine. The rocks are of varying grayish hues, but those in and close to the water wear robes of bright green moss. At first the water appears motionless, lying in a series of diminutive pools, but gravity pulls the water along, forming a pristine mountain stream with tiny pools and riffles.

Within a few hundred feet, the stream flows into an ancient beaver meadow; though the beaver are long gone, the trees have yet to reclaim the meadow and return it to the forest. Native brook trout have remained in the waters of the meadow for generations, sporting their beautiful colors, which artists have painted, and poets have praised.

Farther downstream, perhaps a mile or so, a new beaver dam is found. Here the beaver attempt to recapture the forest and turn the trees back into meadows. But the remote, inaccessible nature of the land meant that few people, including the Catskill region's original Lenape inhabitants, witnessed this on-going, generational work. As a result, there was no known name recorded for the stream, and early colonists called it the Beaverkill, from the numerous beaver colonies found along the headwaters.

Amidst the rugged mountainous landscape lie Alder, Beecher, and Balsam Lakes, all within a mile or two of one another, with each maintaining its own individual, reclusive characteristics. Each has an outlet stream, and for thousands of years, rains and melting snows have eroded the thin, rocky soils, carving deep crevices down the mountainsides, allowing these streams of rapid descent to find their way to the Beaverkill and nourish it with clear, well-oxygenated water, as well as adding native brook trout that flourish in these cold mountain streams.

The lakes are found in the town of Hardenburgh, Ulster

County, and dating back to the earliest days of record, each had a reputation of having an abundance of brook trout, with Balsam Lake maintaining a seemingly inexhaustible supply of the native fish. Access to and from the lakes was difficult and was generally gained by entering from the north through the Mill Brook Valley along unmarked trails that were crude, steep, rocky, and perilous.

Beecher Lake was originally known as Thomas Lake and is found in lots 37 and 38 of Great Lot 9, Beekman Tract of the Hardenbergh Patent. The lake is a spring fed cold-water lake of 19.2 acres, and of the three lakes, Beecher has the highest elevation, at 2,760 feet. Secluded and sheltered by the three mountains of Mill Brook Ridge, Beecher Lake offers serene natural beauty and picturesque views of mountainsides covered by forest greenery in summer; unrestrained colors of red, orange, yellow, and greens in autumn; and dazzling white blankets of snow in winter.

The earliest-known settlement along the upper Beaverkill took place at a site called Quaker Clearing, near where Beecher Brook, the outlet of Beecher Lake, enters the Beaverkill. Local lore proclaims that the first colonizers to enter this region, once called "Big Woods," were a few Quakers by the name of Smith who cleared about 100 acres along the Beaverkill. It is believed they came from Connecticut before the 1820s, sometime shortly after the Revolutionary War. Little else is known about this early settlement, and one day they reportedly gathered their possessions and mysteriously disappeared; likely the result of having to deal with poor soils for cultivation, severe winters, and killing frosts that could appear at almost any month of the year; the same conditions that deterred the Lenape.

The first to write about Beecher Lake, when it was still known as Thomas Lake, was the Catskill naturalist and nature essay writer John Burroughs. Burroughs spent his childhood years growing up on the family dairy farm in Roxbury, Delaware County. Located at the extreme head waters of the East Branch of the Delaware River, there were multiple streams within walking distance of the farm that contained native brook trout.

As a youngster Burroughs learned to fish for trout from his maternal grandfather, Edmund Kelly, and he became familiar with the riffles and pools of streams with names such as Meeker Hollow, West Settlement Stream, Hardscrabble Creek, and Montgomery Hollow. These boyhood streams lured him, often on his way to and from school and at times so much so that he skipped school entirely.

Though there was no fishing on Sundays, Burroughs admitted that during his boyhood years he carried a "fishline" in his pocket and cut a "pole" from the woodlands. His father disapproved of Sunday fishing, "but he was human, and if I brought home several nice trout his reprimand wasn't severe. The trout appealed to him, and he never refused them as tainted flesh."[1]

From a hilltop known as "Old Clump," near the family farm, young Burroughs could view in the distance the summits of many of the mountains in the Catskills. "Old Clump used to lift me up into the air three thousand feet and introduce me to his great brotherhood of mountains far and near, and make me acquainted with the full-chested exhilaration that awaits one on mountain tops. Graham, Double Top, Slide Mountain, Peek O' Moose, Table Mountain, Wittenburg, Cornell, and others are visible from the summit."[2]

As he grew older, he learned that these mountains were the source of famous trout streams known as the Beaverkill and Neversink Rivers, and Esopus, Rondout, and Willowemoc Creeks.

No doubt he thought of fishing these streams, but they were far off, located in a wild, unbroken forest that was barely inhabited and contained numerous deer, bobcats, bears and mountain lions.

As an adult, Burroughs expanded his angling experiences, and he began making camping and fishing journeys into the far-off mountains. He was an early explorer of the upper Beaverkill region, and among the first to write of his camping and trout fishing experiences.

He made his first camping trip in July of 1860, and in a letter describing the expedition, he wrote: "Tomorrow we start for the region of trout and deer. We intend to camp in the woods far beyond any settlement, for two weeks, and live on game."[3] Burroughs was twenty-three years old at the time, and he and a friend hiked to the source of the Beaverkill and fished and camped at Balsam Lake.

Several years later, in June of 1868, Burroughs and a pair of angling companions made a "trouting excursion" to what was then still called Thomas Lake; his goal was to gather information for an article for the *Atlantic Monthly* which he would later title "Birch Browsings."

He described the region as sparsely settled where one may get a view of genuine backwoods life. He wrote of the many cold-water trout streams of rapid descent that have as their source small lakes and copious mountain springs. Burroughs mentioned the abundant wildlife, especially black bear, and noted that deer were becoming scarcer. He related that over the past winter nearly seventy deer were killed on the Beaverkill alone and claimed that the great attraction "is the brook trout with which the streams and lakes abound."[4]

The party traveled up to the head of the Mill Brook Valley on the north side of Mill Brook Ridge where they left their team of horses at a farmhouse. While there, they met a former soldier of the

*Approaching Beecher Lake.* LEE VAN PUT

Union Army who was willing to guide them to Thomas Lake—he had been to the lake the previous winter and knew the way.

Loaded with backpacks, firearms, and fishing tackle, they hiked to the summit of the Mill Brook Ridge overlooking the Beaverkill Valley and, upon arriving there, the veteran who was acting as guide left them, saying that from there on they would have no difficulty finding Thomas Lake. But they did have difficulty and became lost and turned around, then discovered they were back in the Mill Brook Valley. They retraced their steps back up the mountain to the place where the guide had left them, but by that time it was late in the day, and they had to spend the night in the woods instead of at the lake as they had planned.

Burroughs and his companions started out again at dawn through the trackless forest and turned up near Alder Lake. The men became lost and confused and were about to scrap their plans altogether when Burroughs convinced them to stay. They decided to split up, with Burroughs going off on his own. The plan was that if he found Thomas Lake, he would fire three shots; if not, he would fire twice, and the others would answer.

He departed and went ahead and eventually found the lake; he fired his gun three times but received no response; he fired again but still received no answer. Believing he had come a long way, he started back and fired at intervals, and at last he rejoined his friends. Then, everyone became lost again, and Burroughs claimed "I would have sold my interest in Thomas's Lake at a very low figure. For the first time, I heartily wished myself well out of the woods. Thomas might keep his lake, and the enchanters guard his possession! I doubted if he ever found it the second time, or if anyone else ever had."[5]

The party finally did arrive at Thomas Lake and found a

crude raft of logs to fish from. They fished with flies, but no trout were rising, and they caught only a dozen and a half. This was disappointing, since they had been told a week earlier that three men had taken—in a few hours—all the brook trout they could carry, enough that they shared them with neighbors.

Burroughs decided to try his luck in the stream that was the outflow of the lake. It looked more promising than it was; however, he returned to camp with a very respectable number of trout. At sunset he fished the inlet of the lake, where the water was colder than the outlet and the trout were more plentiful. In the morning he started again for the inlet and went far up the stream toward its source, writing "A fair string of trout for breakfast was my reward."[6]

Prior to submitting the article, he wrote a letter giving a brief description of the journey: "we had done some fearful marching, had been lost two or three times, but found the lake and tasted its trout. Tuesday night we got home. I am in hopes I can make a piece of it— 'Among the Birches.' At any rate, it was fruitful to me in much besides trout."[7]

While the trip to Thomas Lake did not go as planned, it did prove to be the basis of an article titled "Birch Browsings." The piece was published in the *Atlantic Monthly* magazine in July of 1869.

Burroughs would go on to make many trips into the mountains and try his angling skills along all the fabled trout waters including the Rondout, Esopus and Willowemoc Creeks, and the Beaverkill, Neversink and smaller Catskill streams.

His favorite waters were the small mountain streams found deep in the forest— "Civilization corrupts the streams as it corrupts the Indian; only in such remote woods can you see a brook in all its original freshness and beauty. Only the sea and the mountain

*Overlooking Beecher Lake.* Lee Van Put

forest brook are pure; all between is contaminated more or less by the work of man."[8]

John Burroughs would become one of America's most famous naturalists. As a writer, his style was unique and focused on the Catskills, its natural beauty, bird life, wildlife, and trout fishing. His adventures were primarily featured in books and in *Century*, *Atlantic Monthly*, and *Scribner's* magazines.

A month after the publication of "Birch Browsings," James Spencer Van Cleef, an enthusiastic trout fisherman, conservationist, and prominent attorney from nearby Poughkeepsie, purchased a large portion of Great Lot 9, Beekman Tract, in the Hardenbergh Patent, which included Thomas Lake and Balsam Lake and a portion of the headwaters of the Beaverkill.

A year earlier, in 1868, Van Cleef had acquired Sand Pond, a body of water known for its population of large brook trout that often reached weights of two or three pounds. The *Ellenville Journal* once reported that a party of anglers from that village caught a large number of trout and graded them to size—the first thirty averaged two and a half pounds! As with Balsam Lake and Thomas Lake, Sand Pond was deep in the forest, far from civilization, located at the headwaters of Willowemoc Creek, where roads and even trails were scarce. Because of its large brook trout, Sand Pond was often the target of illegal netters, who raided the deep-woods pond and removed large quantities of its trout.

After purchasing Sand Pond, Van Cleef placed ads in local newspapers announcing "the pond generally known as Sand or East Pond" was now posted, and trespassing and fishing were forbidden. Another item also announced that a group of sportsmen from Poughkeepsie planned to create a trout preserve at Sand Pond for their own private use during the summer. These men constructed a lodge and obtained leases on four miles of the nearby Willowemoc Creek, forming the Willewemoc Club, the first organized fishing club in the Catskills. Two years later, the club purchased Sand Pond from Van Cleef and renamed it Lake Willewemoc.

Van Cleef believed the best way to preserve trout waters from overfishing and restore streams to their former productivity was through the control of private fishing clubs, and the best way to accomplish that goal was through the purchase of sensitive properties along streams and lakes. In a short time, he and other members of the Willewemoc Club acquired vast tracts of land surrounding the headwaters of the Beaverkill, and Balsam Lake and Thomas Lake. In 1883, they founded the Balsam Lake Club; and after they constructed a lodge, or clubhouse, their trips to and from Sand Pond became less frequent. The area around Balsam Lake and the Beaverkill River has since become a destination for those seeking peacefulness, solace, and good fishing.

# 2

## A Celebrated Family and the Early Years

Thomas Lake was renamed Beecher Lake by James Beecher, who believed that he had discovered the lake while trout fishing the Beaverkill with his brother Thomas. James was the son of Lyman Beecher, a prominent theologian, educator, and reformer, and one of the best-known and most influential clergymen of his day. It has been written however, that Lyman Beecher's greatest legacy may have been the family he produced, fathering thirteen children, including seven sons, all of whom followed their father into the ministry, the most famous being Henry Ward Beecher.

Henry Ward Beecher was an antislavery leader and one of the most conspicuous figures in the public life of his time. For nearly half a century, he was the pastor of Plymouth Church in Brooklyn, and it was there that he "fearlessly preached freedom for the slave" and that his words "electrified a continent and sent a thrill to the heart of the whole English speaking race."[9] He was known throughout America for his support for the abolition of slavery, and when Abraham Lincoln visited New York and was asked what he would like to see, he chose Plymouth Church, where Henry Ward Beecher delivered his famous antislavery sermons.

Of Lyman Beecher's daughters, three also became active in public service: Isabella fought for human suffrage; Catharine fought for educational reform for women; and Harriet Beecher Stowe, perhaps the most notable of the family today, a social reformer and abolitionist who wrote *Uncle Tom's Cabin* (1852). Considered a protest novel, the book forever changed how Americans viewed slavery and became a runaway best seller, with 300,000 sales the first year in the United States, eventually becoming the top-selling novel of the 19th Century.

Lyman Beecher also enjoyed trout fishing; he had fished since boyhood and passed along his knowledge of fishing to his children. Henry Ward Beecher was known as a lover of the trout rod as well, and on occasion penned an article praising trout fishing.

An often-told story of Lyman Beecher and his trout-fishing experiences describes an occurrence shortly after he had become a Doctor of Divinity. One Sunday morning as he crossed a trout stream on his way to church, he saw a large trout clear the water. He remembered he had left a pole and tackle under the bridge, and he leaped down the bank, grabbed the rod, and landed the speckled beauty.

Fishing was generally prohibited on Sunday, as were other amusements, to encourage church attendance. Reverend Beecher, now behind schedule, hurriedly slipped the trout into the tail pocket of his ministerial coat, ran to church, and mounted his high pulpit out of breath. His face was flushed, and his tie askew as the bell stopped tolling. Perhaps in an effort to erase from his mind the fact that he had broken the law and fished on a Sunday, he forgot about the trout he had caught and had hidden in his pocket. The following Sunday morning, when his wife opened the closet door to retrieve and brush his ministerial coat, she smelled the fish before she found it.[10]

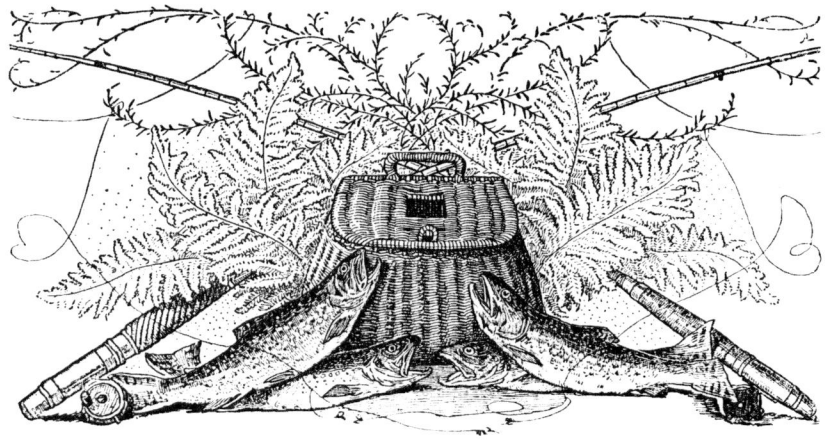

James Chaplin Beecher was born in Boston, Massachusetts, on January 8, 1828, the youngest son of the Reverend Lyman Beecher and Harriet Porter Beecher. Harriet Porter was the daughter of a prominent Portland, Maine, physician and was the second wife of Lyman Beecher, who had nine children with his first wife, Roxana Foote, who died in 1816. The following year he married Harriet Porter, and the couple had three children, Isabella, Thomas, and James.

There was a significant age difference between the two sets of children that distinctly set them apart, causing the three younger children to form a close bond with one another. That closeness strengthened when their mother died at the young age of forty-five; at the time Isabella was eleven, Thomas nine, and James just seven years of age. Before her death, their mother placed with Isabella the responsibility of taking care of little James, and that closeness would last for rest of their lives.

It was not long before the children had a stepmother; Lyman Beecher married a widow from Boston named Lydia Beal Jackson, who brought along two children of her own and added them to the Beecher household.

James Beecher grew up in the shadows of a father and brothers and sisters who became famous as preachers and teachers, all of whom were constantly in the news and the public eye. To follow in the footsteps of his older siblings was not an easy task, and James was reportedly impulsive and "a man of action, not doctrine."

He entered Dartmouth College at the age of sixteen, and being somewhat rebellious by nature, resisted authority. His studies did not go well, and letters from the president of the college to his father indicated that James was short on discipline and needed guidance, but the president believed he would straighten himself out. Nevertheless, during his junior year, he was suspended for failing, having unpaid bills for board, and for being absent for two weeks—time he spent visiting Boston. When he was asked by a relative why he was suspended, he answered, "To give my class a chance to catch up with me."[11] However, James was readmitted to Dartmouth, improved on his studies and attendance, and graduated in 1848 at the age of twenty.

James Beecher had always known that it was his father's desire that he should follow the profession of his father and six brothers and become a clergyman. However, he had had enough of schooling for a while; he had a passion for the outdoors and desired a more adventurous life. Shortly after graduating from Dartmouth, he wrote to his father telling him that he was going to sea to become

a sailor. Coincidentally, James's older brother, the famous Henry
Ward Beecher, also had a strong desire to go to sea, but did not
follow his inclinations.

James Beecher became a sailor on merchant ships involved
in the East India trade, serving on the *Sam Russell*, a clipper ship
out of Boston, one of the finest and fastest sailing vessels ever made.
Clipper ships were long and narrow wooden vessels with large
canvas sails; at the time, they were considered the fastest ships on
the seas. The word "clipper" was said to have originated from the
word "clip," meaning to move at a fast pace.

Tea from China tended to lose its flavor rapidly when it was
stored in the hold of a ship. However, this was not the case with
clipper ships, due to their faster deliveries. James visited various
ports in the Far East and as he gained experience as a sailor, he rose
through the ranks quickly and was promoted to a ship's officer.
He also served on another world-renowned clipper ship, the *N. B.
Palmer*, which was named after the explorer, sailing captain, and
ship designer, Nathaniel Palmer. James was at sea for five years, and

*N. B. Palmer.*

his experience was unequal to anything he could have received on the mainland. He loved being a sailor.

When James Beecher had first arrived in China in 1849 his ship visited Whampoa anchorage, a harbor used by early European and American traders near Canton. While there he went to see a friend of his father's, Catharina Van Rensselaer Bonney, who resided in Canton. They spent a pleasant day together visiting pagodas, and afterward, Mrs. Bonney wrote that James "has a vein of his father's versatile wit and good humor." She also must have noticed that he had the same talents as his father, because she added: "How much good for God he might accomplish with his silver tongue if consecrated to such labor."[12] Perhaps she also planted an idea in the mind of the youngest Beecher that he might one day act upon.

# 3

From Clipper Ship to Pulpit

On a return trip from China, James was asked what he would
like to do next, and he was quoted as saying, "Oh I shall be a
minister. That's my fate. Father will pray me into it!"[13] He stopped
sailing in 1853 and was eager to start a new phase of his life. At
the time, he was described as "a handsome, blue-eyed youth with
golden brown hair, a bronzed complexion, and a tremendous store
of experience."[14] He returned to Boston, the place of his birth, and
tried for a short time the trading business. In September, he married
Anne E. Morse, a widow from Newburyport, a small coastal city
northeast of Boston, who had a young child.

A year later, James Beecher entered Andover Theological
Seminary and began studying for the ministry. Even though he
longed for an outdoor life and enjoyed physical work, he always
knew deep down that he would be influenced by his father and

brothers and become a minister. His brother Thomas had predicted James would "reenter the fold," though there would continue to be restlessness within him. Nonetheless, he attended Andover from 1854 to 1856 and was ordained a Congregational clergyman on May 10, 1856.

The Reverend James C. Beecher did not quite follow the same path as his father or brothers, though. Upon graduation, he decided to devote his ministry to his brethren of the sea, and was appointed as seaman's chaplain for Whampoa anchorage, now known as Pazhou Island, by the American Seamen's Friend Society on the Pearl River at Canton, China. James was well aware of the hazards sailors faced when on the open seas, along with the moral dangers they were subject to when they visited port cities involved in the East India trade, such as Hong Kong, Canton, and Macao. Having had seafaring experience, he was eminently qualified to preach the gospel among sailors, and he began serving on a "floating Bethel;" a place of worship for seamen. It was believed that sailors felt more comfortable on a floating chapel that moved with the tide.

Along with his wife, Anne, and small daughter, Reverend Beecher arrived at Canton on September 3, 1856. The chaplaincy had been unoccupied for nearly two years before he took possession of the floating chapel, but when he began holding religious services, attendance increased dramatically, along with donations to improve the facility.

While there was still a large fleet of ships at the Whampoa anchorage between Macau and the city of Canton, it had been reduced, along with the commerce in and around Canton. Unfortunately, these were unsettling times in China, and the Beechers were at Whampoa for only a few months before hostilities erupted

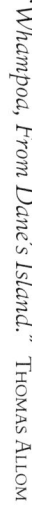

*"Whampoa, From Dane's Island."* Thomas Allom

between China and Great Britain in what became known as the Second Opium War. The war arose when China attempted to stop the opium trade and to halt the greatly increasing numbers of opium addicts in China. Great Britain exported opium grown on plantations in India and sold it to Chinese merchants, who in turn sold the drug inside China. The British used the profits of the sale of opium to buy Chinese goods, such as porcelain, silk, and tea. Great Britain demanded that China open all its ports to foreign trade, exempt British goods from Chinese import duties, and legalize the importation of opium. This greatly alarmed Chinese officials, leading to the war.

Although many ships were in the process of leaving, Reverend Beecher stayed on the Bethel until December 24th, when the last ship in port at Whampoa had left. He and his wife were then forced to abandon their chapel home and sailed for Hong Kong. As soon as he found shelter for his family, he returned to Whampoa to guard the floating Bethel against looters and destruction. When the conflict started, numerous musket balls whistled over his head, though he escaped getting shot or wounded. However, his safety became perilous when a cannonball went through the Bethel's two bedrooms, and then decided it was time to leave for Hong Kong. In January, he learned that the Bethel had been totally destroyed.

During his time in Hong Kong, Reverend Beecher began preaching Sunday mornings on board the decks of ships in the harbor, and in the afternoons, he held services in a small chapel erected among the boarding houses and brothels of Victoria, an urban settlement of the island. Despite drawing good attendance from boardinghouse owners and boarders, Beecher was disappointed with the small number of sailors who came to his services. The chapel he was using was located in the most undesirable part of the city, and each day he had to walk along public streets past brothels and prostitutes who lined the sidewalks. He described the place as "a horrible locality—in which every other house is a shop at the bottom, a brothel upstairs."[15] The new preacher was greatly bothered that every sailor he invited to attend his church had to pass by these "vultures" before they could reach his chapel door. He saw firsthand how sailors were preyed upon and how their weaknesses were exploited; they were robbed and even murdered.

In addition, he experienced up close how lives could be altered by drug addiction, filth, and disease. On the one hand, he understood how shore-bound sailors, looking to forget the perilous conditions of life at sea, could succumb to the temptations of those who prodded them to engage in the excessive vices of alcohol, drugs, and prostitution. Yet Reverend Beecher was charged with providing a safe haven for sailors that included spiritual inspiration and, at times, food, shelter, and a place to read and write.

While at sea on a clipper ship, he had endured watching the moral suffering and sacrifices made by sailors, and he had witnessed firsthand how a sailor's indiscretions on shore often led to their being out of work. Beecher began to believe he was failing in his duty, and the terrible conditions he found at the inner-city location were depressing. Discouraged by what he saw every day, he decided to abandon worship at the location and to put all his time and energy in building a new floating Bethel to replace the one he had lost. In this, Beecher faced obstacles that other missionaries rarely faced, but he persevered and "showed a dedication and fortitude not surpassed by any Beecher."[16]

By November, Beecher's situation improved; through the generosity of merchants, sea captains, and sailors, he was able to build a floating Bethel at Hong Kong that included space for his family. He began preaching at the new facility and enjoyed doing so. At times, he drew capacity crowds, and his sermons were said to be more like those given by his father than those by any of Lyman Beecher's other sons. He also began visiting sick seamen at the nearby Roman Catholic and English hospitals.

In addition to assisting with the chaplaincy, Anne Beecher began the publication of *Hong Kong Monthly Magazine* during the summer of 1857, which was aimed at the English-speaking population of the region.

Encouraged by his success, Reverend Beecher desired to construct a chapel and sailor's home on shore, believing the government would give the land and perhaps even contribute to the construction. He told friends that should this happen, he would consider making China his home for the rest of his life. He saw a greater opportunity in China than he could find anywhere else— "There is a wider field here than I could find elsewhere, not for popularity, but for honest quiet work."[17] He did express concerns that his new Bethel was not safe from the Chinese government, and that the elements could destroy the floating chapel.

He continued to preach to large congregations, and he held evening meetings on the upper decks of various ships, where he would maintain social conversations, read the scriptures, and have prayer meetings. His concerns about the floating chapel proved accurate, and misfortune struck during the stormy season, when five separate typhoons inflicted heavy damage to the Bethel. Once again Beecher was able to raise funds to rebuild the vessel, and soon the number of parishioners equaled the number prior to the disastrous typhoons. He continued to spend his days visiting the sick, holding prayer meetings, preparing for Sunday sermons, and answering correspondence.

When Reverend Beecher visited ships, he appreciated meeting the crews and praying in the forecastle, and he was always received with kindness and respect. The activity that he enjoyed the most was reading and explaining the scriptures and participating in social conversations and prayer. He loved to pray from the pulpit and by the sick, but his favorite place was kneeling by a sailor's sea chest, which held their personal belongings and was the closest thing to personal space on board a ship. While visiting, he would remember his sailing days; he understood the feelings of the sailors who knelt with him, and he envisioned that he was praying with shipmates. He believed prayer "hallowed the place, and somehow purified it," and he pondered that later, when the men were far at sea, the sailors would remember that each "had knelt by his chest, and perhaps in time of trial kneel there again."[18]

*A sailor's sea chest was the closest thing to personal space on board a ship.*
CLIFFORD W. ASHLEY

The Reverend Beecher's concerns over the Bethel again proved to be valid; from July 27, 1859, and for the next six weeks, five massive typhoons swept the area, sinking and damaging ships or sending them onto shore.

Much to his amazement he was able to weather the first typhoon, but the second, in August, removed the upper roof, railings, cupola, and all attachments, almost sinking the Bethel. Again, he made repairs as best he could and held services on Sunday without interruption. On July 29, the Bethel was struck by another typhoon; the rough seas caused the floating chapel to take on water, and it was feared another blow would sink the boat. But having been a sailor, he had no fear, and again Beecher patched up the Bethel and held services on Sunday to a packed house. The following day, the Bethel was struck by the most disastrous storm of the season. Many ships were damaged, but to the astonishment of all, the Bethel held its own. Everything in the lower rooms was floating, but the three anchors held to the floor of the sea, and pumps kept the vessel afloat.

For three nights, Beecher remained soaked from the heavy rain; half his books and clothing were also wet, and he did not sleep. He became distraught and remembered his concerns about the Bethel and his desire to build on shore—in his mind, all of this could have been avoided. He believed he was nearly back to the point where he had started two years ago.

At the end of the year, Beecher longed to return to Whampoa to a new chapel; the fleet there was larger than before the war, and he received many invitations to return. There were times when he thought his life was one of loneliness and that his ministry was not fruitful, yet he continued to try to make a difference, laboring at his post, overcoming obstacles and discouragements.

Adding to his grief was the departure of his wife, Anne, who returned to America for health reasons. With the help of James's older brother, the Reverend Thomas K. Beecher of Elmira, and his sister Isabella, Anne Beecher entered Gleason's Sanitarium in Elmira, New York. James expected his wife to return, but soon learned that she was addicted to alcohol and was not coming back to Hong Kong. This was very troubling, not only to James, but to the whole Beecher family, who publicly promoted a high moral character.

James wanted to believe his wife would return, but he admitted in a letter to his sister Isabella that he was not surprised to hear about her drinking, though he defended her, writing that the past three years had been filled with sorrow and hopelessness: "I testify to the love and devotion of my dear wife, and never has my love changed. . . . If I have suffered, she has suffered more, for it was the thought that her fearful weakness was breaking my heart which gave her greater agony than even her own danger of destruction."[19] He also added that he missed her, but believed Anne was better off in America.

In February of 1861, the Reverend James Beecher resigned from his position as chaplain of the American Seamen's Friend Society. He decided he would leave China, though those most familiar with his work saw his leaving as something he really did not want to do. His last year had been an improvement over the previous years, and even he believed his services were needed more than ever. Nevertheless, Anne weighed heavily in his decision, and with the absence of his wife, he was compelled to leave China. Before leaving Hong Kong, he had the floating chapel moved back to Whampoa.

James had been out of the country for five years, and during the years he was a missionary in China he had faced many challenges and danger. He had anguished over the difficult conditions he found there, but with dedication and fortitude, he had labored on. Throughout his service he had experienced more successes than failures, and these experiences eventually helped him achieve his goal of becoming a dedicated Congregational minister. James sailed for New York in May of 1861. The Civil War had begun one month earlier, and some believed James Beecher returned to America to enlist in the Union Army.

*James Beecher.*

# 4

---

*From Pulpit to Parapet: The Start
of the Peninsula Campaign*

The American Civil War commenced on April 12, 1861, and by the war's end more than 620,000 soldiers had died, totaling more Americans killed than in World War I, World War II, the Korean War, and the Vietnam Wars combined.[20]

Shortly after arriving in New York, the Reverend James Beecher, at the age of thirty-three, enlisted on June 20 for a three-year period as a chaplain with the 1st Long Island Volunteers. Organized in Brooklyn, the 1st Long Island became the 67th New York Volunteer Infantry in September, and their first assignment was the defense of Washington, D.C.

While stationed near Washington, James answered a letter he had received from his sister, Harriet Beecher Stowe, in January of 1862. He indicated that in some respects, he had been very pleasantly situated in China, though upon his return to America, he "found a place in the Army at once and went with it." He wrote that he greatly appreciated her letter and that no one else had written to him or seemed even to care about him: "So I said, well the folks have all forgotten me and my only real friends are in China. Under these circumstances I was just fit for a soldier."[21] He also wrote that there was a rumor that his regiment would soon be going on an expedition in the South. He wished to get closer to the front lines, and was urged to resign his chaplaincy and accept command of a rifle company consisting of men chosen from the regiment. Reverend Beecher did relinquish his chaplaincy, and being assigned to active duty, he became a captain in the 67th Infantry Regiment.

The rumor of heading into the South turned out to be correct; the 67th Regiment, commanded by Colonel Julius W. Adams, became a part of the new Army of the Potomac under General George McClellan. The 67th was assigned to the 2nd Brigade, 1st Division, IV Army Corps and proceeded to Fort Monroe, Virginia, to participate in what was to be known as the Peninsula Campaign. The first large-scale offensive in the Eastern Theater, the goal of the Peninsula Campaign was the capture of Richmond, the capitol of the Confederate states.

In March, the Army of the Potomac began its advance up the peninsula between the York and James Rivers; on the fifth of April, Union forces, including the 67th Regiment and Captain Beecher, met up with Confederate forces who were in defensive fortifications at Yorktown. The two factions fought an artillery duel, but Union officers were unable to gauge the strength of the enemy and advised General McClellan not to launch an assault. After a standoff of several days, Union soldiers probed a section of the Confederate line, but failed to exploit their initial success during the attack, causing further delay. General McClellan believed he was facing a much larger force of Confederates than he actually was, and he spent more time preparing for a siege with a massive bombardment that was to begin on the fourth of May. However, the night before the big event, the Rebel forces slipped away in the evening and headed westerly toward Williamsburg.

Confederate General Joseph Johnston did not wish to make a stand at Williamsburg, nor, for that matter, at Yorktown. His goal was to slow down the Union Army so that the fortifications in and around Richmond could be improved and he could get his men there to assist in the defense of Richmond.

The first battle of the Peninsula Campaign occurred at dawn on May 5, in a driving rain, when Union soldiers ran into Confederate troops near Fort Magruder at Williamsburg. U. S. cavalry, artillery, and infantry drove Rebel skirmishers back to their fortifications, which were commanded by General James Longstreet. As the battle intensified, several units of Confederate soldiers that were retreating toward Richmond did an about-face and returned to aid General Longstreet, who was in charge of the rear guard.

The 67th New York Volunteer Infantry Regiment was active in the siege of Yorktown and the battle for Williamsburg, although we have no account of Captain Beecher's role in it. In a chaotic and bloody struggle, victory favored neither side, but at a critical moment, General Winfield S. Hancock formed his men into a line of battle hurriedly, ran to the front, and yelled "Call to charge." A loud cheer ascended from the line, and five thousand bayonets were readied, as the men swept across a small ravine and drove the enemy in confusion from the field. This was the first bayonet charge of the campaign and the first successful one of the war. "The troops at that time had never seen a bayonet charge; yet Gen. Hancock had confidence in his men, and boldly took the chances."[22] For the first time ever, Union soldiers—Hancock's men—captured a Confederate battle flag. General McClellan stated in a report that General Hancock had participated in "one of the most brilliant engagements of the war."[23]

*"Battle of Fair Oaks."* ALONSO CHAPPEL

During the night, the Confederates quietly abandoned the Williamsburg line. In ten hours of sustained combat, the U.S. Army had 456 killed, 1,410 wounded, and 373 missing; on the Confederate side 1,570 were killed and wounded, with 133 missing. The 67th New York Volunteer Infantry Regiment suffered no losses in the pursuit of Confederate troops at the battle for Williamsburg, but this would quickly change. The next time the regiment met the Confederates, it was in a major clash known as the Battle of Fair Oaks, also known as the Battle of Seven Pines, in Henrico County,

Virginia. The conflict went on for two days and was an important early battle in the Civil War.

On May 31, 1862, Confederate General Joseph E. Johnston, who was still retreating toward Richmond, attacked two Union corps that appeared to be isolated south of the Chickahominy River, a tributary of the James River. The Confederate attacks drove back the IV Corps, which included Captain Beecher and the 67th Regiment, inflicting heavy casualties. Reinforcements arrived on both sides, and as more troops were added to the battle, the Confederates continued their assault while the Union soldiers held their position.

Attacks by the Rebels continued with little effect, and Union forces' counterattacks were also repelled. Eventually, the Confederates withdrew back to the city of Richmond and protected the city from being captured. The leadership of the Federal troops made a fatal mistake by allowing the Rebels to withdraw without a fight. The Battle of Fair Oaks was considered tactically inconclusive, and it revealed the inferior leadership on the part of some Union generals.

In a letter to his sister Isabella, dated June 7, James Beecher recounted his role in the battle. He writes that on May 31, there was an attack by Confederate forces that surprised the soldiers forward of his position, who retreated quickly through his unit "like sheep" with exaggerated stories of their defeat. James was riding as colonel's aide when the colonel ordered him to halt the retreating troops and rally them back into a fighting force. He then went to the front line with his own men. For an hour and a half, they were exposed to intense artillery fire.

When the regiment to his right began to retreat, Colonel Adams requested that Captain Beecher ride down to see if they were being outflanked. He hurried down "on the jump" and rode straight into the enemy, who was coming up the road and through a swamp. He described his situation in a letter to Isabella:

> At least a hundred shots were fired at me but, riding back we wheeled on right doing so as to emplace the road. The bushes were so thick that we couldn't see the enemy until within sixty or seventy yds. & then we opened on them. There were four Regts. engaged, and we only mustered 500 men, one company being absent. We fought well. How I came out I know not. My boys were falling like leaves. Then it became evident that the enemy had got past our flank & were coming round to surround us. The order was given to fall back, we did so. Then called again to the colors & fought till our battery was safely retired, & then sulkily & unwillingly fled out & retired to the rifle pits a short distance in the rear. "<u>The enemy did not follow</u>."[24]

Beecher continued: "As soon as we had retired I went to work with the wounded, was up all Saturday night, Sunday and Sunday night." On Monday they went back to the battleground and found their dead: "Why thirty-three of my brave boys lie there under that ground and one hundred & thirty-six wounded have gone to hospital, and this out of 500 engaged we don't count up on '<u>missing</u>.' All who are not killed & wounded are in the ranks again."[25]

In the front of the "fighting ground" in a sixty-yard area, Beecher counted over thirty "Rebels" and an officer of the 2nd New Hampshire Regiment. He told Isabella that he only wished that in case he was killed, he could have testified to the bravery of his boys and the "desperate fight they made."

*"Charge of General Sickles' Brigade upon the rebels at the Battle of Fair Oaks."*

He complained bitterly about the surprise attack and how the officers at the top of the command did poorly in leading the troops in the battle. He wrote of huge trenches being filled with Rebel dead and the sorrow he felt for his own men:

> From a space ½ mile square 1,173 dead Rebels have been gathered, a fearful harvest. And yet I grieve some over my thirty-three slain than glory over the thousands of the enemy. I saw them fall many of them I knew just where to look for when the battle was done. Poor fellows! & yet I think more sorrowfully of those they have left behind. Yesterday I was distributing the mail & it all came back upon me, for letter after letter was for someone whose eyes would never read more.
>
> Ah well, so the world goes. Orders came to fall into line. The enemy are not far off. It may be that in an hours' time we go through the furnace again. I only wish the Northern slavery politicians were in <u>our</u> front rank, or in the first rank of the enemy I care little which.[26]

Combat during the Civil War was often up close; soldiers fought mostly on foot, in tight formations, and in large-scale battles. They fired their weapons at close range, with bullets and cannons firing grapeshot, which caused most of the bloodshed. As the war continued, more accurate and deadlier rifles replaced muskets, and over one million Americans were killed or wounded, about one-third of all who served in the war. Soldiers often viewed the aftermath of a battle as being even more horrific than the actual battle, "describing landscapes so body-strewn that one could cross them without touching the ground."[27]

The Battle of Fair Oaks was considered one of the bloodiest of the war; in two days of fighting, there were 13,736 casualties, consisting of 5,739 Union soldiers and 7,997 Confederates. It was the first large scale offensive of the Eastern Theater and marked the end of the Union's advance on Richmond.

# 5

---

## *The Battle of Malvern Hill*

On July 1, 1862, the Army of the Potomac participated in the Battle of Malvern Hill, including the 67th New York Infantry Regiment, which was in the thick of the fight. Located near the Confederate capital of Richmond, Virginia, Malvern Hill had extremely steep, wooded slopes on its southern and western sides, while its gentler northern slope was a broad, open wheat field. General McClellan recognized that the site would give a great advantage to defenders, and it was here he chose to halt his retreating army and invite the pursuing Confederates, led by General Robert E. Lee, to engage in battle.

Malvern Hill was two miles north of the James River, and its location gave excellent fields of fire to the defenders. The slightly sloping fields of wheat were in front, causing any Confederate attack to take place over completely open areas.

General McClellan placed a great deal of his artillery at the crest of the hill, facing in three directions, with almost 70,000 infantrymen in support, most of whom were held in reserve behind the crest. Along the eastern front were elements of the II, III, IV and VI Corps under the leadership of Generals Sumner, Heintzelman, Couch, and Franklin.

"*The Army of The Potomac—Our Outlying Picket in the Woods.*"
WINSLOW HOMER

Generals Lee and Longstreet believed that they might breach the Union line with artillery fire, followed by a speedy and strong infantry attack, though they recognized that the Army of the Potomac held a commanding position. The Confederate bombardment failed; however, the infantry attack was carried out anyway, with twenty separate brigades advancing across the open fields.

The Union artillery dominated, and most of the attacks fell well short of the hill's crest. Repeated attacks also failed, and a large portion of the Confederate army was defeated. The effect of the Union artillery was said to be "murderous." Union troops mowed down wave after wave of Rebel soldiers, and at times intense hand-to-hand combat ensued, but the enemy was repulsed when Union reinforcements arrived. Confederate General D. H. Hill led a gallant attack that was rendered partly fruitless by a lack of support; he was quoted as saying, "it was not war, it was murder."[28] At the end of the battle, there were slightly more than 5,000 Confederate soldiers killed or wounded and 3,000 Union troops injured or killed in battle.

The Union forces at the battle of Malvern Hill were mostly made up of regiments from New York, New Jersey, and Pennsylvania, with the 67th New York Volunteer Regiment once again in the thick of the fight. Captain James Beecher saw heavy fighting in the Peninsula Campaign in Virginia. Actively involved in five months of continuous combat, he faced battle admirably, despite harrowing experiences. It had been said that he was a good preacher; after his military experiences, it was added: "but he fought better than he prayed."[29]

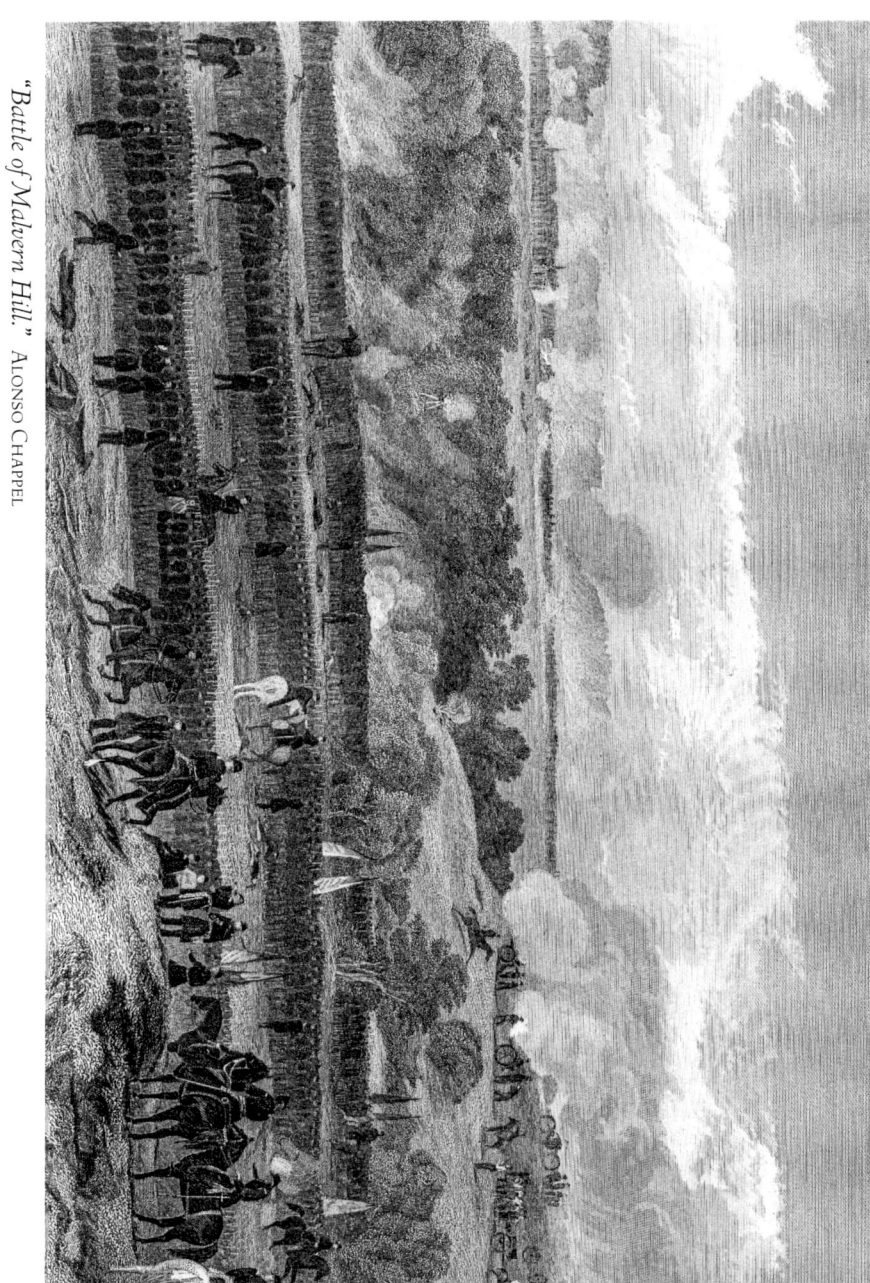

"Battle of Malvern Hill." ALONSO CHAPPEL

# 6

## James Takes Poor Advice

In early September of 1862, Captain Beecher's brother, the Reverend Thomas Beecher, enlisted in a newly formed regiment that he helped recruit, known as the 141st New York Infantry. The regiment was made up of three companies from Chemung County, which included Elmira, and was considered a "home regiment," meaning it was made up of men who either knew or were related to one another.

Thomas, who was the regimental chaplain, urged James to leave the 67th Regiment and join him with the 141st. James agreed to do so, and on September 8, Captain James Beecher received a discharge from the 67th at Yorktown, Virginia, and joined the 141st Regiment as a lieutenant colonel on October 14, 1862.

Prior to this event, the 141st Regiment had left New York State for Washington, D.C., and there had been growing tensions between Thomas Beecher and Colonel Samuel Hathaway, the

commander of the regiment. Thomas was critical of Colonel Hathaway's abilities as a soldier and questioned whether the colonel was
capable of leading the regiment. The two men's dislike for one
another escalated when Thomas personally interceded on James's
behalf and succeeded in getting James the commission and appointment to the regiment as a lieutenant colonel. The regiment already
had a lieutenant colonel, who was now displaced, causing the other
officers in the 141st to resent both Beechers. They particularly did
not like the way the previous lieutenant colonel was treated, and
they blamed Thomas and resented James.

To make matters worse, Thomas resigned in January, after
serving a little over four months, leaving James in a difficult position. He was accused of plotting with Thomas against Colonel
Hathaway and was now left on his own to deal with the anger and
resentment of the colonel and the other officers.

As soon as Thomas left, the officers held a meeting where
they accused James of being a liar and told him that the honorable
thing to do would be for him to resign his commission. He thought
about resigning, but he had received a telegram from Thomas
urging him not to, because, Thomas reasoned, if he resigned, it
would appear to be an admission of guilt and proof that Thomas
had falsely accused Colonel Hathaway. Regimental politics were
not the only unpleasant events occurring in James Beecher's life
at the time. Anne's alcoholism was getting worse, and James had
begun a personal relationship with Frances B. Johnson, of Guilford, Connecticut. Unlike Anne, Frances was a stable and religious
woman.

Unable to resign and alienated from his fellow officers,
Lieutenant Colonel James Beecher, now thirty-five years of age,
became bitter and withdrawn. He was overcome with grief over

what occurred within the regiment. At the time, he was proud to be a soldier and had extensive combat and military experience. He was irritated by regimental politics and his involvement with them and, coupled with the fact that reconciliation with his wife seemed to be growing more and more hopeless, he began to drink to excess. Because he had trouble sleeping, he took chloroform, and an army surgeon gave him morphine, which sent him to the hospital. Charges of incompetency and drunkenness were brought against him, and it was rumored that he would soon be facing a court-martial.

*James Beecher.*

Having been informed of this possibility, James's sister Isabella intervened on his behalf and visited the Beechers' family friend, Secretary of War Edwin M. Stanton. She pleaded with Secretary Stanton to grant James an honorable discharge, which he did on March 7, 1863. Because he was experiencing what appeared to be mental health issues, James opted to stay with Isabella and her husband, John, in Hartford, Connecticut, and he began to make plans to divorce his wife. However, he received word in April that Anne had died of delirium tremens, which is often caused by withdrawal from alcohol.

Isabella took James to New York City for treatment and placed him in the Taylor Institute of the Swedish Movement Cure. The institute was run by the brothers George and Charles Taylor, who were physicians specializing in therapeutic exercises and orthopedics and in the Swedish Movement Cure, a method that used exercise and massage to cure disease. Patients were given several exercises relative to the afflicted area and then were shown how to stretch and bend the body.

James Beecher stayed at the Taylor Institute for two weeks, and while there, he was visited by his friend, Frances B. Johnson. During this time, he admitted he took the chloroform in an attempt to commit suicide, and he was still talking about wanting to die and to cease troubling his friends. His sister Isabella thought he should live in the New York or Connecticut area and return to the pulpit, but James wanted to return to the army. His sisters were opposed to the idea, and Isabella claimed he was worn down with sorrow and anxiety. Against the advice of his sisters Isabella and Catharine, James Beecher did rejoin the Union Army.

# 7

## A New Beginning: The 1st North Carolina Colored Volunteers

In July of 1862, Congress authorized President Lincoln to use black troops, though this policy was not pursued until the Emancipation Proclamation on January 1, 1863. The proclamation declared "that all persons held as slaves" within the rebellious states "are, and henceforward shall be free." The proclamation was a giant step in allowing black men to serve as soldiers in the Union Army and Navy. Many black men saw military service as a chance to participate in an army of liberation, and by the close of the Civil War, nearly 200,000 black men fought for their freedom and the United States.

John A. Andrew, a prominent antislavery lawyer and then governor of Massachusetts, acted quickly and recruited the 54th and 55th Massachusetts Infantry Regiments, which were primarily made up of black soldiers. The 54th was the first Northern regiment to be formed of *free* black men. Fathers and sons enlisted together, and though some enlistments came from slave states, others came from Indiana, Ohio, New York, and even Canada. Two of the most famous men to enlist were Charles and Lewis Douglass, the sons of Frederick Douglass, the famous orator, writer, and leader of the abolitionist movement. Charles and Lewis lived with their father in Washington, D.C., but traveled to Massachusetts to join the 54th Infantry in April 1863. According to his service record, Charles transferred to the 5th Massachusetts Cavalry to become its first sergeant. Lewis was the sergeant major of the 54th and was wounded in the assault on Fort Wagner. (The 54th Massachusetts was featured in the 1989 Academy Award–winning film *Glory*. The film recalled the famous regiment and their assault on Fort Wagner on Morris Island, South Carolina.)

When Governor Andrew was assembling the regiment in the Boston area early in 1863, he approached Captain Robert G. Shaw, a captain in the 2nd Massachusetts Infantry Regiment, one of best veteran regiments, about leading the 54th Massachusetts. At first, Shaw turned down the governor, because he was reluctant to leave the 2nd Massachusetts and was unsure that he could handle the responsibility or if he could live up to everyone's expectations. He then reconsidered, believing that his mother would be hugely disappointed in him if he did not accept the position; his parents were strongly opposed to slavery. Shaw accepted the position on February 15 and came to Boston to assist in forming the regiment.

Robert Gould Shaw was born in Boston on October 10, 1837, to a prominent abolitionist family. He was home-schooled, studied abroad, was admitted to Harvard College in 1856 at the age of nineteen, and attended Harvard from 1856 to 1859. Not sure of what he intended to do with his life, Shaw dropped out of Harvard before completing his studies.

Shortly after the start of the Civil War, Shaw enlisted as a second lieutenant in the 2nd Massachusetts Infantry Regiment and experienced combat during the Shenandoah Valley Campaign and the Battle of Antietam. He exhibited courage and composure under fire, and even though wounded, Shaw, at the time a captain, decided that he would stay in the Union Army until the war was over.

*Colonel Robert Shaw.*

After joining the 54th Massachusetts, Shaw was promoted to colonel, and during February and March of 1863, he organized and drilled the new recruits near the city of Boston. He was a strict disciplinarian—he wanted the men to become good soldiers so that more would follow. In the beginning, Colonel Shaw did not see his men as individuals; he was only twenty-five years of age and lacked experience in working with members of a different race. But by the end of March, he had gained knowledge and saw that many of his men were intelligent and educated, and he began to admire them and the ease with which they adjusted to military life. He began treating his men with more respect, and in return, they respected him.

With two regiments secured, Governor Andrew wrote to Secretary of War Edwin M. Stanton detailing his plans to form a brigade of black troops that would also include former slaves living in Federal-occupied eastern North Carolina. Union army forces had seized New Bern and the surrounding areas the year before, and slaves had greeted the Northern soldiers as liberators. As the word spread, thousands of slaves migrated to this coastal community, located at the confluence of the Trent and Neuse Rivers.

Governor Andrew thought that the recruitment of black soldiers would be aided if he sent part of one of his black regiments to North Carolina; he believed black men would be hesitant to join white units, but once they saw a black regiment, they would be more eager to enlist. The Governor also believed that the officer who would lead the black troops should have intellectual and moral qualities, as well as abolitionist sentiments and military experience. To lead the black brigade, he selected Colonel Edward A. Wild, a steadfast abolitionist who had proven military experience. Shortly after being chosen, Colonel Wild was promoted to brigadier general.

On April 13, 1863, the War Department authorized General Wild to raise a brigade of North Carolina volunteer infantry to serve for three years. This was one of the first attempts by the Federal government to enlist ex-slaves in the defense of the Union. Black soldiers truly fought for their own freedom, and by the end of the war, black recruitment would become widely accepted. North Carolina would provide more than 5,000 of the 179,000 black troops raised.

*"The escaped slave in the Union Army."*

While black regiments had been formed previously, they had been made up of mostly free blacks, and the question remained whether a black brigade could be mustered from recently freed black slaves. It was believed that the success of the recruitment depended greatly on the leadership of General Wild and on his careful selection of officers for the 1st North Carolina Colored Volunteers, which, it was hoped, would serve as a model for future black regiments.

Edward Wild had earned a medical degree from Harvard and had studied medicine in Paris. At the beginning of the Civil War, he had enlisted as a combat officer, preferring to lead troops rather than to treat their wounds. He was a captain in the 1st Massachusetts Infantry Regiment, fought in the Peninsula Campaign, and was wounded at the Battle of Fair Oaks. As a colonel, Wild was wounded even more seriously during the Maryland Campaign and lost an arm while leading the 35th Massachusetts Infantry Regiment.

General Wild's goal was similar to that of Governor Andrew's; he desired to select intelligent officers with moral qualities who were both ardent abolitionists with military experience and who would travel to North Carolina with him to assist with recruitment. As colonel for the first regiment, he selected James C. Beecher of Hartford, Connecticut. James had all the requirements Wild was looking for: he had battle experience with the 67th New York Infantry and with the 141st New York Infantry as a lieutenant colonel, and he believed strongly in abolition, having come from a family of fervent abolitionists.

James Beecher was an excellent choice to lead a black regiment. "Though Wild could not have known at the time, by selecting Beecher, he chose a man who staunchly would defend his men and, upon occasion, all people of color against unfair treatment by whites."[30] On May 18, General Wild, Colonel Beecher, and other officers selected by Wild were in New Bern, North Carolina, with the goal of recruiting black soldiers from the slave population of the region. They had barely been there a week when they learned from a *Wilmington Journal* report that the Confederate Congress had passed a law in early May dealing with black soldiers and their white officers. The law stated that all black prisoners of war would be subject to the laws of the state in which they were captured and would be treated as slaves engaged in an insurrection, and "All commissioned officers, who shall be captured in command of negroes, shall suffer the penalty of death."[31]

Colonel Beecher established a recruiting office on May 21, 1863, chose antislavery men to serve as officers, and went to work filling the ranks of the 1st North Carolina Colored Volunteers. He then selected a site on the south side of the Neuse River for a camp, and in the evening, he took over the first squad of recruits and cleared enough brush to erect seven tents. As additional men enlisted, more land was cleared, more tents were erected, and a parade ground was constructed where these soldiers made rapid progress in drill. Colonel Beecher did not have a chaplain in the regiment, and in addition to his duty of teaching his men to be soldiers, the former army chaplain decided he could take over the

*Infantry Camp circa 1863.*

spiritual care of his men, as well, and he served as the regimental chaplain and commanding officer. He quickly formed a special relationship with his men.

The liberated slaves joined the regiment at a rate of 200-300 a week after passing a physical by Assistant Surgeon Dr. Daniel Mann. Dr. Mann questioned many as to why they wanted to enlist and received replies that focused on "duty."

In a letter to family friends dated Sunday, June 7, 1863, Colonel Beecher wrote of the initial trials of his new black regiment. The former army chaplain reminisced:

> Had service at 6 P.M., before dress parade. I formed the battalion into close column by division; then, having no chaplain, gave out, "My country, 'tis of thee." We have some sweet singers among the officers, and many of the soldiers sang too. Then I read the 34th Psalm, and they seemed to feel it's import— "The Lord is nigh unto them that are of a broken heart." This poor man cried and the Lord heard him. Then I prayed with them. I had given no directions, but they knelt down and bowed their heads—near 700 men. It affected me beyond measure, and I prayed for them in faith. When I spoke of their past lives, of their having been bought and sold like brutes, of their wives and children not their own, of their sorrow and degradation, many wept like children. I know not that I ever felt the reality of prayer more deeply, or more enjoyed speaking face to face with Him who loves all of us, but especially is tender to the down-trodden and oppressed.[32]

In a letter dated June 14, 1863 and published in an abolitionist

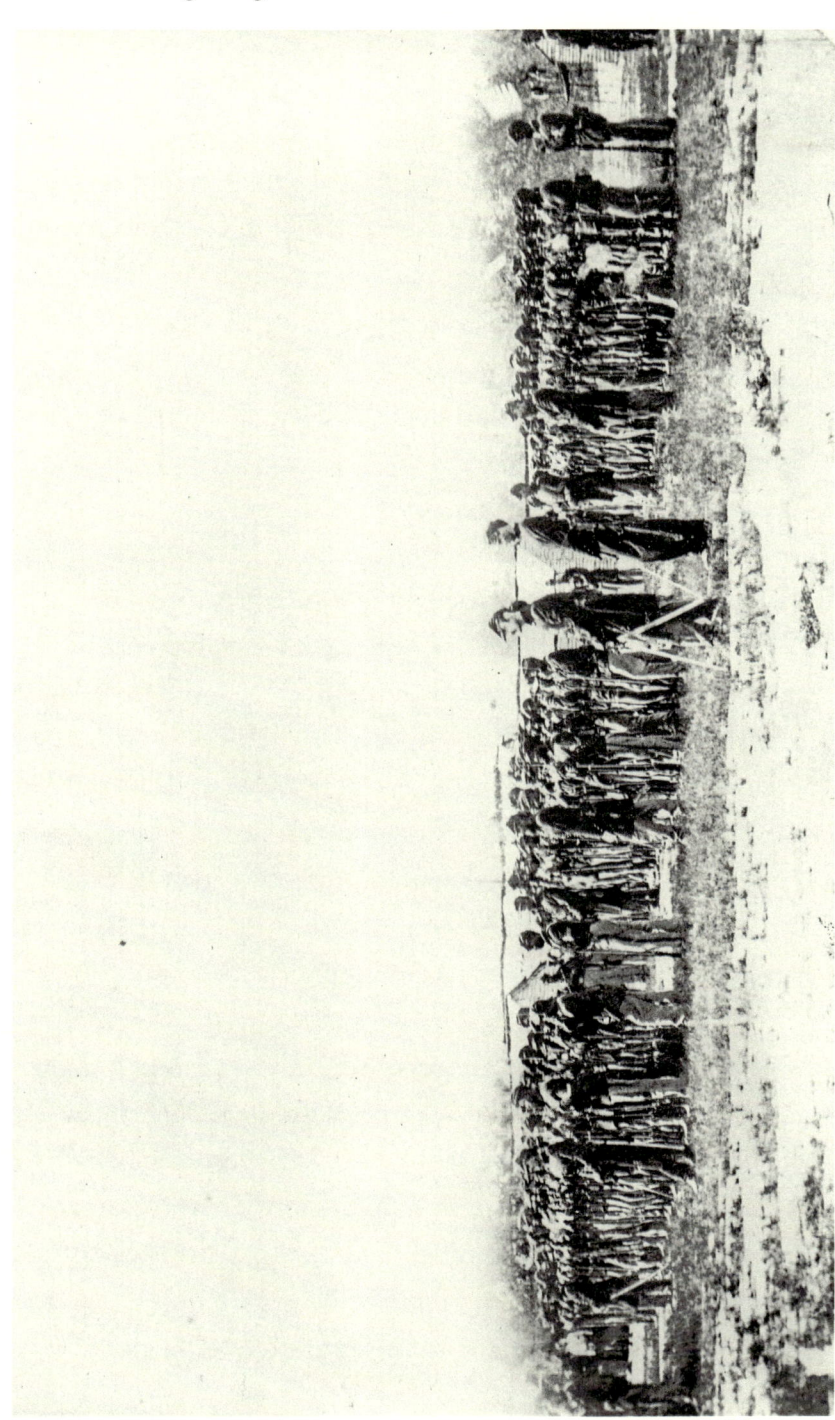

"1st U.S. Colored Infantry."

newspaper in Boston titled *The Liberator,* Dr. Mann wrote of the establishment of the 1st North Carolina Colored Volunteers and the appointment of Beecher and other officers— "Of our Colonel it is enough to say that he is a Beecher, (Rev. James C.) to show that he *chose* his position, and did not *drift* into it. Our captains and other line officers are men of like character, who have deliberately sacrificed much, as the world counts sacrifice, in accepting their present positions."

Dr. Mann also praised General Wild and Colonel Beecher:

Gen. Wild lost an arm, and was otherwise severely wounded at Antietam. Colonel Beecher, though hitherto unwounded, has braved dangers and borne labors which few men have the luck to find the power to endure. In the campaign of the peninsula, though, like the lamented Fuller, he was ever foremost in the fight, and when the battle ended, the most faithful and indefatigable in caring for the wounded, working at one time thirty-six hours without rest to save the suffering and soothe the dying. Of our captains and lieutenants, all have seen service, and several have lost an arm or hand, or bear the marks of other severe wounds.[33]

The men were quick to learn military drill, and Colonel Beecher and the other officers were impressed with their skills. They took great pride in how fast the men were becoming an organized military unit. The progress that the former slaves made as soldiers astonished Colonel Beecher, and he wrote to friends that every day he experienced new attributes that pleased him. He added that he greatly enjoyed preaching to the men and would gladly lead them in battle; they were the best he had ever seen. Beecher claimed the regiment was disciplined better than any other that he knew of and that their efficiency was second to none. By the middle of June, he wrote: "In spite of my hard work, I'm becoming somewhat of an enthusiast—I wish doubtful people at home could see my three weeks regiment. They would talk less nonsense about negro inferiority. Our discipline today better than that of any regiment I know of, and I believe, by the blessing of God, our efficiency will be second to none."[34]

Toward the end of June, Colonel Beecher wrote to Frances Johnson, the young woman from Guilford, Connecticut, whom he had been seeing when he stayed with his sister Isabella in Hartford. He told her that his regiment was now organized, equipped, and properly drilled and added that after his experience with the squabbling and politics he had experienced with the 141st New York Regiment, he was happier than he had been in months.

Colonel Beecher also decided to teach the men in his regiment to read and write. After 1830, many Southern states instituted laws prohibiting slaves from learning to read and write. Through letters to the *Liberator*, a prominent abolitionist newspaper published in Boston, he requested that he would be happy to receive from the good people of Massachusetts simple reading material that he and other officers could use to teach the former slaves.

He also wrote that his new regiment might soon be involved in freeing slaves on some of the large plantations. The idea of a Beecher leading black troops in the South was considered a powerful symbol, and James was clearly aware of its implications; he writes and tells Frances that if he lives, he hopes to be as well known in North Carolina as any public figure: "It will make the

*Union Soldiers circa 1863.*

chivalry a little riled to have one of my name traveling about, but if
God gives me life, and strength, they shall hear of me often enough
to become used to it."[35]

Before they left New Bern the 1st North Carolina Colored
Volunteers participated in a raid at nearby Kenansville, Duplin
County. The target of the raid was a Confederate arms factory that
produced swords, bayonets, lances, and Bowie knives. The regiment
engaged with Confederate pickets at several locations, damaged a
railroad, burned the factory to the ground, and rescued three black
prisoners from a courthouse. While the raid was fairly insignificant,
the new regiment had ventured into enemy territory where slavery
still existed and had gained some confidence.

By the middle of July, about two months after the first man
enlisted, Colonel Beecher believed that his regiment could do well
in battle. At the time, the 1st North Carolina Colored Volunteers
were joined by the 55th Massachusetts Volunteer Infantry. The
55th Massachusetts, also a black regiment, was formed in May
from the overflow of troops that made up the 54th Massachusetts.
Beecher believed that the troops of the 55th Massachusetts were

better clothed and equipped, and he noted that they had a full staff of officers, which Beecher saw as a great advantage. He also believed that as soldiers, his men were their equal. Black regiments were generally ill equipped and were often given weapons of poorer quality, at times outdated, that used different types of ammunition. Of real concern to Beecher was the fact that his men received $7.00 per month, and the 55th Massachusetts nearly double that, at $13.00 per month.

Before leaving New Bern, the black women of the community presented a flag of regimental colors to the 1st North Carolina Colored Volunteers. Colonel Beecher's sister, Harriet Beecher Stowe, assisted in creating the flag of dark blue silk, fringed with gold, with a goddess of Liberty trampling a serpent on one side; on a scroll held by the goddess was written "First Regiment North Carolina Volunteers" and "a rising sun with the word LIBERTY above it in immense crimson and black letters, and below the inscription 'The Lord Is Our Sun and Shield.'"[36] On the staff appeared a silver flashing that was engraved "From the Colored Women of New Bern to the 1st N.C.C.Vols."

The presentation of the flag occurred on the Fourth of July, 1863, and the *New York Times* reported that the regiment was drawn up into a line, and the flag presented to General Wild, commander of the brigade. Then the flag was given to Colonel James C. Beecher, commander of the regiment, who handed the flag to the standard bearer, and with fanfare and emotion, Beecher said:

In all these years of war and death, of dark clouds, lighting occasionally, at last there comes sunshine—a glorious sunshine, gilding the clouds, and over the top of it appears the magic word Liberty. Thank God, now the word has meaning. Two hundred thousand men like unto you rally now to the cry. This is the flag we fight under—fight for liberty, not for one, but for all, as God has made them. We bear it henceforth our rallying point. This flag will show us where to rally. Let it be sacred, and its influence will grow stronger day by day. I deliver to you as the most sacred trust that has ever passed through my hands since I was born. I will devote myself to it, and you, I believe, will follow it with a single heart and a strong mind.[37]

The regiment proudly carried the flag when it marched out of New Bern on July 30, 1863. Colonel Beecher had received orders to fortify the forces near Charleston and embarked for Folly Island, a barrier island just south of Morris Island, near Charleston Harbor, South Carolina. In August, the 1st North Carolina Colored Volunteers and the 55th Massachusetts, with a small detachment of the 2nd North Carolina Colored Volunteers, formed a brigade that participated in the siege of Morris Island and Fort Wagner.

# 8

---

*Colonel Robert G. Shaw,*
*the 54th Massachusetts,*
*and the Battle for Fort Wagner*

General Quincy Gillmore was assigned to lead the campaign to capture the City of Charleston. Supported by naval warships, General Gillmore planned to capture Morris Island and place heavy guns on Cummings Point that could destroy the Confederate forces at Fort Sumter. After that occurred, the army and navy could move swiftly to seize Charleston, the birthplace of the War of the Rebellion. Fort Sumter had been a federal facility held by the U. S. Army in the middle of Charleston Harbor, and its capture by the Confederates on April 13, 1861, was the start of the Civil War.

Morris Island was a barrier island along the Atlantic coast. Together with Folly Island, James Island, and Coles Island, they were strategically located between the Stono River and Charleston

Bay. On July 10, 1863, Union troops landed on the southern tip of Morris Island, under the command of Brigadier General George C. Strong. Prior to their landing, Union artillery on Folly Island along with naval gunfire from warships bombarded Confederate defenses that were protecting the southern end of Morris Island.

*Morris Island with 6 monitor-class warships offshore, including the* USS New Ironsides *(far right) actively firing.*

As General Strong's brigade moved forward, they received heavy artillery fire that included shell, grape, and canister. However, they still managed to capture several Confederate batteries while they advanced approximately three miles to within range of Fort Wagner. The fort, located in the middle of the island on the ocean side, was a massive Rebel stronghold made of sand, earth, and logs, and guarded the approach to Charleston Harbor.

The only way to approach the fort on land was across a narrow stretch of beach with the ocean on one side and a swampy marshland on the other. The following day, June 11, General Strong led his brigade, including the 7th Connecticut Infantry, the 76th Pennsylvania Infantry and the 9th Maine Volunteer Infantry in a dawn attack on Fort Wagner.

The assault failed, and the Union soldiers suffered heavy casualties. That Fort Wagner was strongly defended can be seen in the battlefield statistics—it was reported that Union casualties numbered 339, with 49 killed, 167 missing, and 123 wounded; the Confederates had just 12 casualties.

This precipitated another attack that included a close-range land and sea bombardment, combined with a land assault again led by General George C. Strong and 5,000 infantry soldiers. General Strong was highly regarded as a military officer and for being unselfishly patriotic.

The Confederate fort was defended by 1,620 well-entrenched troops with fourteen heavy guns and mortars. The bombardment began by land and sea on July 18, and this time, the attack would include the 54th Massachusetts, the black volunteer regiment from Boston, commanded by Colonel Robert G. Shaw. Shaw was as determined as anyone to prove that his men could fight in battle as well as white soldiers.

The assault force was formed into three brigades, the First Brigade under General Strong, consisted of the 54th Massachusetts, 6th Connecticut, 48th New York, 3rd New Hampshire, 9th Maine and the 76th Pennsylvania. The Second Brigade was under Colonel Putnam and included the 7th New Hampshire, 100th New York, 62nd and 67th Ohio; and the Third Brigade, which was held in reserve under General Stevenson of the 24th Massachusetts, included the 10th Connecticut, 97th Pennsylvania, and the 2nd South Carolina. The 2nd South Carolina, like the 54th Massachusetts, was a regiment of African American soldiers. There were also four companies of the 7th Connecticut that manned and served the guns on the siege line.

The 54th Massachusetts had an inconceivable journey just to get to the assault site; the regiment departed James Island on July 16 at 9:00 A.M., with only rations of hardtack (cracker-like squares of flour, water, and salt or sugar) and coffee. They marched through the night, arriving at Coles Island at 4:00 A.M. the next morning.

The next day, they were transported from 11:00 P.M. until 4:00 A.M. by boat from Coles Island to Folly Island and breakfasted on the same food as the previous day. They then marched to a point opposite Morris Island and from there were transported by a steamer across the inlet at 4:00 P.M. to begin their march to Fort Wagner.

The men were tired, weary, sleepless, and dinnerless; they had been without proper food and tents during pelting rainstorms for two nights. Upon their arrival at General Strong's headquarters in the middle of the island they were wet, weary, thirsty, and hungry. Colonel Shaw reported to the general at 6:00 P.M., and General Strong informed him that the attack would begin that evening, and that he knew Shaw's men were tired, but he was an admirer of the regiment and its officers and gave them the honor of leading the attack on Fort Wagner. The general believed the 54th was equal to any other troops and "one of the strongest and best officered."[38]

Colonel Shaw sent his adjutant officer to return to the regiment and have Lieutenant Colonel Hallowell bring up the 54th. They arrived at 6:00 P.M. General Strong saw the tired looks on the faces of the men, who had gone two days without rations and had no food since the morning when they began their march, and he wished to feed them, but it was too late; they needed to take their place at the head of the assault.

At 6:30 P.M., Colonel Shaw and General Strong mounted and started toward the front of the column. Shaw stopped and gave letters and papers to a personal friend who had been staying with General Strong. If he did not return, he wanted them to be forwarded to his family.

*Brigadier General George Strong.*

Once the men of the 54th were in position at the fore-front, they were ordered to lie down and rest. Their muskets were loaded, but not capped. They rested for half an hour while the attack column and reserve were placed in position. Colonel Shaw told Lieutenant Colonel Hallowell, "I shall go in advance with the National flag. You will keep the State flag with you; it will give the men something to rally round. We shall take the fort or die there! Good Bye!"[39]

While the men of the 54th assembled on the beach preparing to attack, a paradox must have formed in their minds. They heard the soothing sounds of ocean waves rhythmically falling softly, foaming and hissing on the white, sandy beach. No doubt they also envisioned the horror of the battle that lay ahead, and of being exposed on the open beach, charging into the merciless fire of the enemy.

General Strong, a West Point graduate who had graduated fifth in his class, suddenly appeared before the regiment, mounted on a magnificent prancing gray horse; he was dressed in full dress uniform with white gloves and had a dashing large yellow bandana tied about his neck. He told the men of the 54th that he was from Massachusetts and that he knew they would fight for the honor of the state. He asked the men if they would like to lead the attack on Fort Wagner, and they responded with a loud cheer. He then pointed down the beach and asked, "Is there a man here who thinks himself unable to sleep in that fort tonight?"[40] And the men roared in unanimity "NO!"

The general then called out the color bearer who carried the American flag and asked, "If this man should fall, who will lift the flag and carry it on?" Colonel Shaw, who was standing nearby, stepped forward, and taking a cigar from his mouth quietly said, "I will,"[41] and the 624 men of the 54th Massachusetts responded by cheering wildly: "Both officers were inspired; the siren of martial glory was sedulously luring them to the bloody battle and inhospitable trenches of Wagner. There was a tremor in Colonel Shaw's voice and an impressiveness in his manner. He was young and beautiful, wealthy and refined, and his heroic words soon flowered into action—bravest of the brave, leader of men!"[42]

Before the attack started, Colonel Shaw placed five companies in the first line and five behind. He then walked up and down the line, told them they should prove they were men, and stated that thousands would judge how well they fought. He was said to be composed and graceful as he positioned himself next to the American flag in the first line. He was dressed in a close-fitting officer's jacket with a colonel's silver eagle on each shoulder; he wore light blue trousers with a narrow silk sash around his waist under the jacket, and a felt hat with cord; on his belt was a sword with his initials. The officers shook hands, took out their revolvers, and tightened their sword belts.

The signal was given and Colonel Shaw at front and center called the men to attention; he raised his sword, gave the command "Forward," and started down the beach. The attack was made at twilight, 7:45 P.M. on July 18, 1863, and at first the men marched at quick time, 120 steps per minute, but as they got closer to Fort Wagner, the pace was increased to double quick, 180 steps per minute. At about 1,000 yards from the fort, the enemy opened fire with canister shot, a mass of small iron balls shot from cannons, used to kill foot soldiers. Many were wounded, but the men kept on, not faltering, but cheering and shouting as they advanced. Colonel Shaw gave the order to charge, and the front row lowered their bayonets. When they were within 150 yards, they were greeted

*"Storming Fort Wagner."* Kurz & Allison

with a horrific fire of artillery and musketry that poured down on them from the Confederates, with deadly results, greatly reducing the ranks of the exposed men of the 54th Massachusetts Regiment.

Despite the heavy losses, the 54th surged over sharpened wooden stakes and through a moat filled with water waist deep, and they reached and scaled the earthen parapet; here the Stars and Stripes was planted, and here General Strong fell, mortally wounded. Colonel Shaw, still leading the attack, charged forward and was one of the first to scale the walls, and there he was hit with several bullets and died instantly from his wounds. Hand-to-hand combat ensued, and where the body of Colonel Shaw had fallen, twenty of his men lay dead around him, two covering his body. The 54th descended into the fort and continued hand-to-hand fighting. With nearly all of its officers dead or wounded, the regiment was withdrawn by eighteen-year-old Captain Luis Emilio, who acted as the regimental commander after all other ranking officers had been killed.

Lieutenant Colonel Hallowell, to whom Colonel Shaw gave the state flag, also reached the parapet, where the flag was planted. Badly wounded, he rolled down the slope into the water-filled moat and was then wounded a second time; but with great difficulty, he managed to crawl back to the line. The state flag had been lost to the Rebels, but the national flag had been carried to the parapet by Sergeant Carney, who kept the symbol of the United States high as he charged up the hill urging troops to follow him. Though wounded in the head, right arm, and both legs, he refused to concede the flag and valiantly protected the Stars and Stripes, despite his wounds, and was still able to remove the flag safely from the battlefield. "Carney lost a lot of blood and nearly lost his life, but not once did he allow the flag to touch the ground."[43] Years later

"*Attack on Fort Wagner.*" THOMAS NASH

Sergeant William H. Carney was awarded the Medal of Honor, becoming the first African American to win the prestigious award.

The 54th had heavy losses; and additional assaults by General Strong's other regiments continued the attack, but the Confederate forces repelled everything. At 10:30 P.M., the fight for Fort Wagner ended. The battle was a Union Army disaster; there were 1,515 casualties, and the 54th lost the most: 281 solders, 42 percent of its men. The Confederates had 181 killed, wounded, or missing. The wounded suffered from "bayonet thrusts, sword cuts, pike thrusts, and hand grenades; and there were heads and arms broken and smashed by the butt-ends of muskets."[44] Of the regiment's twenty-three officers, all but eight were killed, wounded, or missing. General Strong died after the battle from wounds he received leading the assault on Fort Wagner; Colonels Shaw, Putnam, and Chatfield were all killed.

When the war began, both Union and Confederate troops used the "minnie ball," as they called it, in their muzzle-loading rifles. A French army officer named Claude-Etienne Minié invented the bullet, which had a conical shape instead of being in the traditional round musket shape. When it struck an arm or leg, the bullet tended to shatter the bone, causing horrific wounds. The bullet was made of lead in .58 caliber, larger than most bullets used today, and had a hollow base at the bottom that was expanded by the

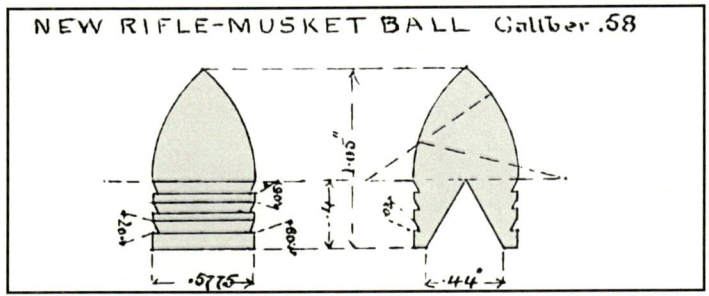

*The "Minnie Ball."*

gases released by the igniting gunpowder when the rifle was fired. It fit snugly into the rifled grooves in the barrel, and its rotation as it came out the barrel of the rifle increased its accuracy to great distances.

Being wounded in a Civil War battle could be devastating; the most common surgical procedure in battlefield hospitals was the amputation of arms and legs, the result of being shot with a minnie ball. A wound from this type of bullet is perhaps best described by Dr. William T. Helmuth in his book *A System of Surgery* (1879): "The effects are truly terrible; bones are ground almost to powder, muscles, ligaments, and tendons torn away, and the parts otherwise so mutilated, that loss of life, certainly of limb, is almost an inevitable consequence."[45]

Dr. Helmuth goes on to write that no one, except those who have witnessed the type of gunshot wounds made by a minnie ball, has any idea of the "horrible laceration" they cause—"The wound is often from four to eight times as large as the diameter of the base of the ball, and the laceration so terrible that mortification [gangrene] almost inevitably results."[46] Often the only way to save a soldier's life was to amputate the limb; tens of thousands were amputated with unsterilized instruments.

After the battle of Fort Wagner, enemy soldiers stripped the bodies of Union soldiers of useful apparel and souvenirs, then piled the dead into mass graves. Colonel Shaw was stripped down to his undergarments; his watch and chain, jeweled ring, sword, and personal papers were stolen from his body in the night after the shooting had stopped. Shaw was singled out for what the Confederates deemed the ultimate insult—burying him beneath his fallen black troops.

Reporting on the battle of Fort Wagner for *Harper's Weekly*, a correspondent wrote that when the assault on Fort Wagner was over, there was the usual truce meeting held with officers from both sides to negotiate the handling of the wounded and an exchange of prisoners. The Union officer was said to have told his Confederate counterpart that the officers and men of the black regiments were to be treated the same as all others, to which the Confederate officer replied that that issue was for his superiors to decide.

This issue was a real concern for the government of the United States and its articles of war. It was feared that black prisoners would not receive fair treatment, and this was evident in how the Rebels purposely, in their eyes, disrespected the body of Colonel Shaw by burying him beneath dozens of his men in a mass grave. Although Rebel forces saw this deed as a final insult to Colonel Shaw, the *Harper's Weekly* reporter asked: "Where else could he be so nobly and fitly buried? With those devoted soldiers of his and of the country, and for them and the country, he faced that storm of rebel fire, and died smiling. Where should he be buried but with them? On all the soil of South Carolina there is no spot so holy and prophetic as that grave."[47]

George W. Williams, a black Civil War veteran and historian, wrote about the battle for Fort Wagner in *A History of the Negro Troops in the War of the Rebellion 1861–1865* in 1888. Williams, too, saw that the Confederate soldiers' treatment of Colonel Shaw's remains had the opposite effect of the Rebels' intentions. Williams wrote of Shaw:

Many brave soldiers fell in the forlorn assault upon Fort Wagner, but when some great painter has patriotic inspiration to give this battle an immortal representation, Colonel Shaw will be the central figure; and America will only remember one name in this conflict for all time to come—Colonel Robert Gould Shaw! This was a noble and precious life, but it was cheerfully consecrated to human freedom and the regeneration of the nation. He had good blood, splendid training, and wide experience for one so young, and had inherited strong antislavery sentiments. When he had fallen, a flag of truce called for his body. A rebel officer responded, "We have buried him with his niggers." It was thought thus to cast indignity upon the hero dead, but it was a failure. The colonel and his men were united in life, and it was fitting that they should not be separated in death. In this idea his father joined, and the following letter exhibits his feelings:

Brigadier-General Gillmore, commanding Department of the South

Sir—I take the liberty to address you because I am informed that efforts are to be made to recover the body of my son, Colonel Shaw, of the 54th Massachusetts Regiment, which was buried at Fort Wagner. My object in writing is to say that such efforts are not authorized by me or any of my family, and that they are not approved by us. We hold that a soldier's most appropriate place is on the field where he has fallen. I shall therefore be much obliged, General, if, in case the matter is brought to your cognizance, you will forbid the desecration of my son's grave, and prevent the disturbance of his remains or those buried with him. With most earnest wishes for your success, I am, sir, with respect and esteem,

Your most obedient servant,

Francis George Shaw
New York, August 24, 1863

Instead of dishonoring the remains of Colonel Shaw by burying him with his brave black soldiers, the intended ignominy was transformed into a beautiful bow of promise that was to span forever the future of the race for which he gave his life. He was representative of all that was good in American life; he had wealth, high social position, and the broadest culture. From his exalted station he chose to fight with and for Negro troops—not only to lead them in conflict, but to die for them and the Republic; and although separated from them in civil life, nevertheless he united the rich and the poor, the learned and the unlearned, the white and the black, in his military apotheosis.[48]

# 9

*"They have been slaves and are just learning to be men"*

While Colonel Beecher and the 1st North Carolina Colored Volunteers did not take part in the attack on Fort Wagner, Beecher did send part of his regiment to Morris Island to work on fortifications outside the fort. They were joined by black soldiers from the 54th and 55th Massachusetts, 2nd South Carolina, and 3rd U.S. Colored Troops. These men participated in "fatigue duty"—constant physical labor—digging trenches for artillery, transporting heavy guns, moving powder, shot, and artillery shells; and they labored at creating parapets, enlarging trenches, and filling sandbags necessary to the operation. The work was hard and tedious and was best accomplished after dark because of sniper fire from sharpshooters and artillery fire from Fort Wagner. It lasted through August and into September.

During this time Colonel Beecher wrote Frances Johnson that he was still on Folly Island, but that he had been to the front along with the sharpshooters at Fort Wagner on nearby Morris Island. He described the fort as a "troubled up mess of sand bags & loose sand mounting 8 or 10 guns, & yet there lie six monitors and huge Ironsides [armored Union warships] & don't dare to come near." He complained that sharpshooters were perched in many different locations at the fort, firing through cracks in every direction, and that the shooting was constant. He claimed that if one were to show only half his head, he would get a ball through it. He had seen a soldier shot through the heart and wrote that he detested this sneaky way of fighting; "I heard enough of that villainous ball whistling on the Peninsula," referring to the battle of Fair Oaks. He stated that they were no closer to taking Charleston than they were six months ago and ended his letter saying, "I feel so peculiarly anxious when my boys are under fire. I'm responsible for everything connected with them."[49]

*Union Camp at Morris Island, 1863.*

The Confederate forces abandoned Fort Wagner on September 7, and because the War Department had not established specific duties for the 1st North Carolina Regiment, the regiment was reduced to doing fatigue duty. What most disturbed the officers of the black regiments was that their troops were also constructing camps, pitching tents, and so on for white regiments who sat around watching them do so. The colonel of the 55th Massachusetts and Colonel Beecher became enraged at the situation, and Beecher fired off a letter on September 13, 1863 to General Wild, protesting how his men were being treated. Stating that he had learned that one segment of his regiment had been sent to nearby Morris Island, where they were ordered to prepare a camp for a white regiment, he sarcastically wrote that he believed white soldiers normally pitch their own tents and construct their camps; but his men had been so busy laboring for other regiments they had no time to make their own camps.

*Building a stockade, circa 1863.*

Beecher was adamant that his troops should not be used as laborers for white soldiers and that this action could have a serious effect on black men, who only a short time ago were slaves. "They have been slaves and are just learning to be men," he wrote.[50] Beecher believed his men were recruited and trained to fight in the ongoing war and that by doing menial work for white soldiers, some of the freedom they were fighting for was being taken away.

General Wild told his colonels to stop performing fatigue duty for white regiments, and he forwarded Beecher's letter to Brigadier General Israel Vogdes, who issued an order banning the use of black soldiers performing fatigue duty for whites.

The digging of trenches and other hard labor had gone on for weeks and left little time for the 1st North Carolina Colored Volunteers to drill or learn to use their guns. They did not once see their weapons during this time and rarely drilled, and then only at night along a moonlit beach. Their guns were three different types of hand-me-downs and quickly rusted from the salt air and lack of use.

Colonel Beecher also made repeated requests for better equipment for his men, who were often short of arms, ammunition, and clothing. He worked tirelessly to put his regiment of ex-slaves on an equality with other Union soldiers. While the men were digging and doing other fatigue duty during the day, at night they eagerly learned how to read and write from the officers of the 1st North Carolina Colored Volunteers. More than 300 learned these skills while on Folly Island. Many soldiers in the white regiments did not know how to read or write.

In December, Beecher made an application to General Quincy Gillmore for new guns and equipment, and the general informed him he would have them. Weeks later, in a letter to

Frances Johnson, he told her he was still waiting. The lack of adequate weapons for his regiment was just one of many issues that irritated Colonel Beecher. He had little faith in working through the proper military channels while trying to obtain proper weapons. Finally, in January of the new year, he decided to write to Henry Wilson, a U.S. Senator from Massachusetts, about the unfair way his soldiers were being treated.

Beecher informed the senator, who was also the chairman of the Senate Committee on Military Affairs, that he was in command of the 1st North Carolina Colored Volunteers, who were mustered into the Union Army on June 30. And he complained that from the beginning of August until December, he never saw his command all together and that it was difficult to continue to train his troops under those circumstances. The reason for this separation, he told the senator, was that after arriving at the barrier islands near Charleston, his regiment was involved in constant fatigue duty of the toughest kind in the trenches on Morris Island, often under heavy fire.

He also wrote that his soldiers were legally formed by an Act of Congress for ten dollars a month, three of which were to be in clothing. They were assured that ultimately, they would be paid the same pay as white soldiers, and they relied on this, not just for the money, but for the sense of "soldierly equality." The men worked hard, were diligent and patient, and Beecher stated: "I most earnestly testify that they have deserved equal pay" and that lesser pay was a constant reminder to his men that they were held to be inferior.[51]

Colonel Beecher ended his letter by writing that many of his men worked for the army as "contrabands" for six to ten months without pay and without vouchers, and that it is doubtful that they would ever be paid for these services; but as soldiers, they "are entitled to prompt consideration."[52] "Contraband" was a term used by the U. S. Army to describe escaped slaves who were affiliated with Union forces, usually as laborers.

In writing about Colonel James Beecher and the special relationship he had with men of his regiment, the *Hartford Evening Press* reported how well the regiment, trained by a "God-fearing colonel, which might literally be said to go to the war with the Bible in one hand and the bayonet in the other, did carry itself in the fight."[53] Actually, the regiment had been in a major battle prior to the newspaper report, but without Colonel Beecher.

# 10

## *The Battle of Olustee*

On February 6, 1864, the 1st North Carolina Colored Volunteers sailed from Hilton Head, South Carolina, for Jacksonville, Florida, where they joined the famous 54th Massachusetts and the 8th United States Colored Troops and assembled with other Union forces in the Jacksonville area under the command of Major General Quincy Gillmore and Brigadier General Truman Seymour.

The Florida expedition was aimed at severing Confederate supply routes of agricultural products, including beef, but also hoped to recruit more men for the black regiments. Two days after reaching Jacksonville, the 1st North Carolina was designated the 35th United States Colored Troops; however, the designation did not reach the regiment until after it participated in its first major battle at Olustee, Florida, about fifty miles west of Jacksonville.

After breaking camp at Barber's Plantation at 7:00 A.M.

on February 20, 1864, General Seymour led the Union forces on a march paralleling a railroad westward toward Lake City. At 2:00 P.M., Union cavalry encountered Confederate pickets east of Olustee. Pickets are generally a small group of about forty to fifty men posted on guard ahead of the main line of defense. General Seymour had a battery of artillery brought up to engage the enemy, and a brigade of Union soldiers attacked the Confederates on their left.

*"Barber's House at the ford on Big Creek, Colonel Barton's Headquarters."*

Unfortunately, the Union cavalry units were drawn into an ambush, and a fierce battle developed near Olustee. The Confederates had constructed strong fortifications at one of the only defensible locations in the area, where the railroad passed through a narrow corridor of dry ground that was bordered by impassable swamps and bays to the south, and by a body of water known as Ocean Pond to the north.

The 7th New Hampshire Regiment took the place of the cavalry at the front, but the troops were hardly in position when they broke and ran. The regiment was replaced by the 8th U.S. Colored Troops, and intense fire from the enemy along with the loss of their colonel, who was killed soon after the fighting started, caused this regiment also to break and bolt to the rear. General Seymour's men were tired and hungry after marching sixteen miles, and as the fighting intensified, both armies added additional troops to the foray. For a time, each side gained and lost ground in what would become the largest battle fought in Florida during the Civil War. However, much to his regret, Colonel Beecher did not participate in the battle of Olustee. Early in February, he had left for Washington with dispatches, once again, to attempt to obtain better arms for his men, and he had placed Lieutenant Colonel William N. Reed in charge before the troops were moved to Florida.

The fighting was severe, and each side suffered heavy casualties. However, after receiving reinforcements, the Confederates began advancing toward the Union lines. General Seymour was present on the battlefield and by late afternoon, he recognized that he could not gain a victory. To prevent a complete rout and to cover his retreat, he requested his last reserves: Colonel James Montgomery's brigade, which included two black regiments, the 54th Massachusetts and the 1st North Carolina Colored Volunteers.

Both regiments arrived at the battle front at 4:00 P.M. The more experienced 54th Massachusetts took the position on the left, and the 1st North Carolina moved directly forward and began to attack, but the enemy had just received reinforcements, and the fighting was fierce. Both Union regiments played an important role in the battle by holding back the Rebels' advance. The regiments ran into heavy gunfire from the Confederates, who held good defensive positions—the closer Union soldiers got to the Confederates, the stronger the enemy fire. Lieutenant Colonel Reed gallantly led the 1st North Carolina in battle, mounted, and with his sword drawn he led the attack against the enemy. Reed was mortally wounded and died several days later at Beaufort, South Carolina.

The intense fighting of the two black regiments allowed the rest of General Seymour's forces to complete an orderly retreat. The general began withdrawing troops to a new line in the rear, and this continued in successive lines of battle. Finally, General Seymour ordered a retreat the following day, and the tired and hungry men of the 1st North Carolina marched thirty miles to their home base.

It was reported at the time that the two black regiments saved the expedition from being a total rout: they "fought like devils," even though the 1st North Carolina lost their commanding officer. They suffered heavy casualties, and after the Union troops withdrew, Confederates murdered almost all the wounded black soldiers and left their bodies unburied.

*"Battle of Olustee."* Kurz and Allison

General John P. Hatch reported, "It is now known that most of the colored men were murdered on the field."[54] Both regiments paid for their heroics: the 54th lost one captain, had two lieutenants wounded, and eighty-four men were killed, wounded, or missing; the 1st North Carolina suffered even more casualties. In addition to Lieutenant Colonel Reed, 199 men and nine other officers were killed, wounded, or missing. Union forces totaled 1,861 killed, wounded, or missing, and the Confederates 946.

Following the "ill-fated" Olustee battle, the 1st North Carolina remained in the Jacksonville area. Colonel Beecher rejoined his regiment in Florida and appears once again to have been unsuccessful in his attempt to secure proper weapons for his men. In a letter to Frances Johnson dated March 16, 1864, he wrote: "I hope the guns for my Regt. will not be delayed. My men fought that fight [Olustee] with guns that the white regiments would not have gone into action with. It is a shame that good men can't have good guns." He ended the letter: "I'm afraid Henry [Wilson] will forget the guns in Washington. I'd give two months' pay to have them here now."[55]

Colonel Beecher's trip to Washington and his experiences there were unsettling. He was despondent, and his lack of success in obtaining proper weapons was deeply disturbing. This event and the fact that he had missed the opportunity to lead his regiment into battle troubled him greatly. In a letter to Frances Johnson, he expressed his disappointment:

> The thought that the very hour I have longed for & almost prayed for ever since I entered the service had come and gone, & that my Regt. the work of days & nights for months, had fought its maiden fight without me. I couldn't bear it, and so the gloomy phantoms of an unsettled mind seemed realities until I was half insane I believe. The moment I set foot in camp again, the surging chaos of my men told how truly they knew me. The load was lifted and after the first sweet icon of joy came terrible thoughts, of my selfishness in thinking of myself while obsessed with you, of my ingratitude to God

*James Beecher.*

in being cast down by one single disappointment, when he had been so good to me in so many ways.[56]

The following day Beecher wrote that the order finally did come for the rifles, as did the commissions for his officers, and that his regiment was now named the 35th United States Colored Troops. He praised the efforts of Senator Wilson and Secretary of War Stanton, whom he had also visited on his trip to Washington.

However, new issues arose. On April 4, Beecher wrote to Frances Johnson that he received a "letter from ordinance dept. at Hilton Head yesterday and they won't issue my guns unless they are sent from Washington and ordered to be issued to my regt., so here comes a month's delay until my letter announcing the fact, gets to Washington, and the arms are ordered sent on. Isn't it hard for a man to keep his temper with such annoyance?"[57] Colonel Beecher had great difficulty with army bureaucracy and paperwork. There was no end to how it frustrated him.

Beecher again wrote to Frances from Jacksonville on April 15, 1864:

By the way, there is now no doubt that all of my wounded men left on the field at Olustee were bayonetted in cold blood.

It is said to have been done by some South Carolina troops. The enemy report only 18 prisoners from my command. At least fifty are known to have been left on the field & at the depots at Sanderson & Barbers Station.

You may judge this does not make me feel peculiarly happy, especially when the new man came to relieve General Seymour, while he pities the poor Loyal Floridians who

Frances Johnson.

suffer so much from the effects of the war.

Don't see anything particularly out of the way in this, says he has no doubt my wounded were murdered, but that it's "very hard to restrain men when their blood is up" etc. etc. If there were but ten stupid Generals in the whole army of the United States, each one of the ten would be assigned to Command a district & there wouldn't be but ten districts made unless an eleventh stupidly could be imported to put in charge of it.[58]

A few days later Beecher wrote to Frances Johnson urging her to come to Hilton Head, South Carolina, and he would meet her there and they could be married.

Colonel Beecher hated any prejudice against the use of black soldiers in the Union army, and he strongly supported the men of his regiment. He wrote again of his confidence in their abilities in a letter to Captain W. L. M. Burger, the assistant adjutant general to General Quincy A. Gillmore, that he believed the men of his regiment had no superiors for marching or fighting. During the month, Colonel Beecher's regiment spent much of its time marching from one post to another, searching for Confederates, raiding and causing havoc, and stealing cattle, potatoes, and horses. On the fifth of May he wrote that he had been steadily marching for eight days and had trekked 115 miles, raiding and hunting rebels, and had "played mischief generally."

Colonel Beecher was still bothered by circumstances he could not control, however. On June 1, he wrote to Frances Johnson: "Everything harasses me. The loss of so many officers and men. The separation of my command. The improbability of getting officers; for the War dept. has not acted on my nominations for promotion for wounded six or eight weeks ago." And in his frustration, he began to doubt his own capabilities, writing, "Perhaps it is my fault, possibly I am not competent to command a regiment, yet in all the past, in respect to the getting arms & equipment & organization of the command I cannot see a single thing neglected, or endeavor unmade."[59]

In view of Colonel Beecher's sensitivity and the difficulties he experienced in the failed attempts to get proper weapons for his men, it is easy to understand his vexations and why he would take these issues personally. This mind-set continued into July, when he was ordered to take his regiment and the 34th United States Colored Troops back to James Island in Charleston Harbor, South Carolina. While there, under the command of General William Birney, they participated in many skirmishes, and on July 7, an angry General Birney wrote to Captain W. L. M. Burger, assistant adjutant general for the Department of the South, that he would attack as soon as Colonel Beecher's regiment received replacement weapons. According to the general, the regiment "numbers only a little over 320 men for active duty; of these ninety are without arms and the rest have four kinds of arms, none of them fit for service."[60] Finally, after constant attempts to secure proper weapons for his men, Colonel Beecher's regiment received new Springfield rifles.

For months, Beecher tried to obtain personal leave time so that he could travel north to Connecticut and wed his fiancée, Frances Johnson. Finally, after repeated attempts, he succeeded in getting Frances to travel to him, believing he would at least be able to meet her at Hilton Head, South Carolina, and they could be married there. Unfortunately, an order had recently been issued excluding women from the southern war zone. Not to be denied, Frances traveled to Washington, D.C., in July of 1864, met with

Secretary of War Stanton, and succeeded in getting a pass that allowed her to travel to Jacksonville, which was then occupied by Union forces.

Frances made plans to travel with friends who would act as escorts or chaperones for a wedding that was seen as very unconventional. On her arrival at Jacksonville, she learned that Colonel Beecher had been sent inland and could not meet the wedding party. Undeterred, Frances, on July 18, traveled up the St. Johns River through enemy territory on a boat that carried troops and supplies to meet her future husband at army headquarters. A military wedding and dinner followed, and Frances was allowed to stay in Florida with her husband. The couple was assigned a house in Jacksonville, though James would be stationed at Baldwin, west of Jacksonville, conducting raids throughout the countryside.

*Frances and James Beecher.*

There were times when James returned to Jacksonville and Frances Beecher would accompany the colonel on horseback while he made his rounds. Years later, Frances would recall that her proudest day while living in the South with her husband was when she rode alongside him during a dress parade: "I saw no regiment more manly in appearance, none with straighter line or better drill, nor any more worthy of their uniform, than that which was then called 'The First North Carolina Colored Volunteers.'"[61]

Throughout the war while stationed at Jacksonville or Beaufort, Frances Beecher, like her husband or other officers of the regiment, spent her mornings teaching the men who were former slaves to read and write. When they had enlisted, only two or three were literate, but they were eager to learn and spent every spare moment at improving their skills. When they were mustered out of the U. S. Army, every one could sign his name to the payroll.

# 11

## *The Battle of Honey Hill*

Colonel Beecher received orders on November 25, 1864, to embark for Hilton Head, South Carolina at 3:00 A.M. with his regiment "rationed and equipped." In addition, the 34th United States Colored Troops and a detachment of cavalry and artillery were also placed under Beecher's command. They became a part of an expeditionary force of approximately 5,000 men led by Major General John P. Hatch that aimed to cut off or destroy a portion of the Charleston & Savannah Railroad near Pocotaligo, South Carolina. It was believed that such an attack would divert Rebel troops from Savannah, and that, in turn, would aid Union General William T. Sherman's forces, who were marching from Atlanta toward Savannah. General Hatch's force was made up of two brigades, plus a naval brigade and portions of three batteries of light artillery.

The Union soldiers boarded various types of boats and traveled about eighteen miles up the Broad River to Boyd's Neck. Other regiments involved in the expedition were the 25th Ohio, 32nd United States Colored Troops, 102nd United States Colored Troops, 127th New York Infantry, 144th New York Infantry, 157th New York Infantry, and the 54th and 55th Massachusetts Infantry Regiments.

After disembarking the men and equipment at Boyd's Neck, the U.S. forces moved inland. On the morning of November 30, they encountered significant resistance from Confederate regulars and militia who maintained a battery of artillery at Honey Hill, near Grahamville. The Confederates were well entrenched, with seven guns that had a commanding view of the road and nearby surroundings; their left line stretched out into pinelands and the right along a fence that skirted a swamp. The 54th and 55th Massachusetts attacked these positions and were met with heavy fire. A correspondent for the *New York Times* described the Rebel fortifications:

> They had also on the outside of their fort a line of rifle-pits from which they poured in upon us a heavy fire, while in the woods on our right, they also had infantry posted, so that as our men advanced they were met by a concentrated fire of musketry from the rifle-pits and the lower front of the fort and the woods, while from the parapet of the fort they were being mowed down by continuous charges of grape and canister. The fire was terrible, but our men stood it bravely and returned volley for volley, while the artillery was rapidly brought into position and the fort was vigorously shelled. A charge was ordered and the Thirty-fifth United States

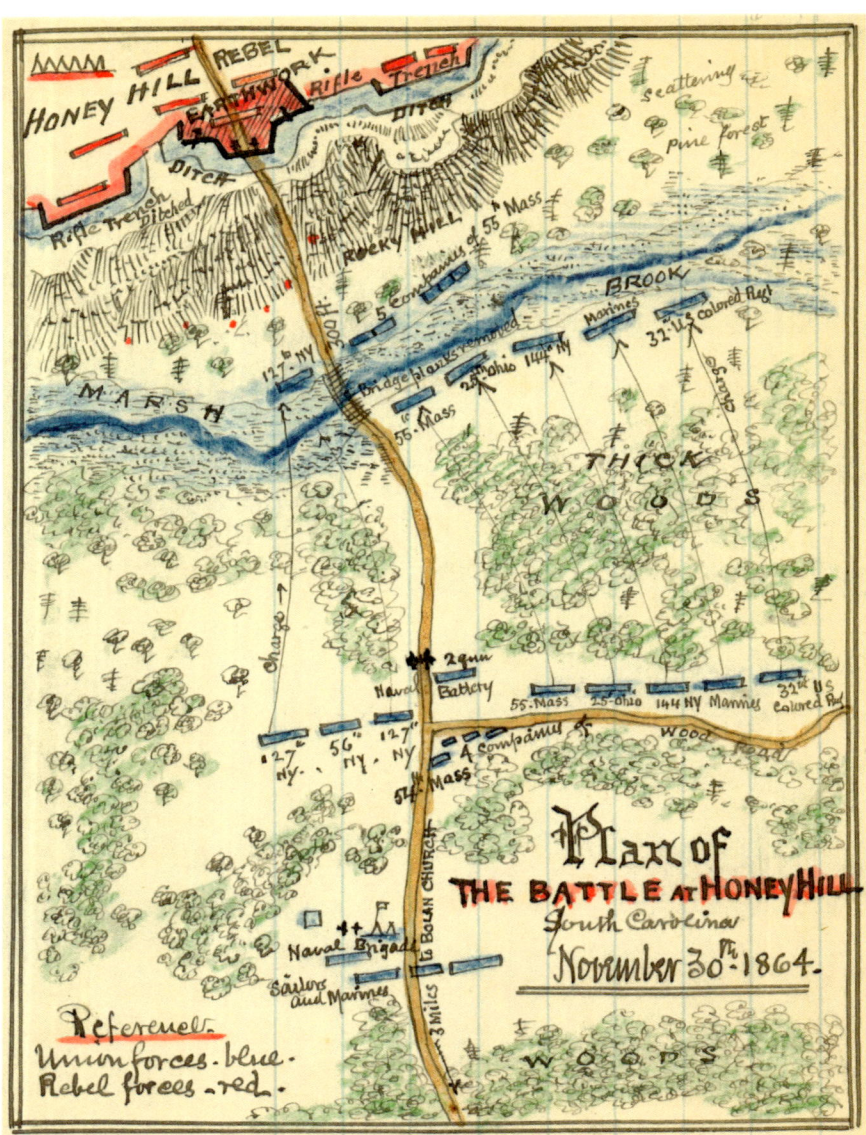

*Plan of the Battle at Honey Hill, South Carlina, November 30, 1864.*

Colored Infantry went in with a cheer. They, however, found it impossible to hold their ground under the tremendously destructive fire, and they were compelled to retire after a gallant fight in which they suffered severely. It was now discovered that there was not solid ground enough to admit of toe [sic] advance of more than a single regiment at a time, and that it was impossible to assault the works from the flanks, owing to the swampy ground. However, regiment after regiment was sent in the hope that they might be able to carry the fort by sheer bull-dog bravery.[62]

The 35th United States Colored Infantry that charged the fortifications "with a cheer" was Colonel Beecher's regiment, and while they had fought at Olustee alongside the famous 54th Massachusetts as the 1st North Carolina Colored Volunteers, this was the first time their beloved colonel would lead them in a major battle.

Colonel Beecher's involvement in the attack has been written about several times. He was severely wounded early in the fight, though he stayed in the field until the end of the day, leading his men in five separate charges. Perhaps the most accurate accounting of the battle is best described by Colonel Beecher himself. In a letter to his wife Frances dated December 2, 1864, he wrote:

Officers Hosp. Ward 6
Beaufort, S.C., Dec. 2nd 1864

My Beloved,

I'm grateful for life spared though very sorrowful at being on my back.

We had a hard fight under great disadvantage. There was only one road, with thick jungle on either side & the enemy had 2 guns right sweeping the road. I was 5th Regt. & was ordered up, to move through the thicket along the right of the road, flank the battery and charge it. I did so, but the enemy ran the guns off, & I came right in front of a strong earth work that nobody knew anything about. A round shot killed poor old Gray. I left him & pushed on at head of my column, a round shot struck me across both legs above the knee & upset me. I found no bone broken & pushed on. Then the boys opened fire without orders, and the bushes were so thick that the companies were getting mixed. I halted and reformed the companies. Then got orders to move to left of the earth work & try to carry it.

I led off by the left flank, the boys starting finely & crying out "follow de cunnel." It was a perfect jungle all laced with grape vines, & when I got on the left of the earth work and closed up, I found that another regiment had marched right through mine & cut it off, so that I only had about 20 men. We could see the rebel gunners loading. I told the boys to fire on them & raise a yell, hoping to make them think I had a force on their flank. We fired and shouted & got a volley or two in return. A rascally bullet hit me just below the groin & ranged down nearly through my thigh. Then I went back with my twenty to the road again, found the 35th, 55th, 54th men all mixed together. Went to work to clean-up, though the fire of the enemy was very hot. Got hit here with a spent ball in left hand.

In course of an hour got the companies all right & in order. Firing ceased at dark, we held our ground. I was so dizzy that I couldn't get along so I shook hands with Col. Willard who did splendidly all day and wasn't touched and Dr. Marcy helped me back the church, then I was sent to the boat & here I am. Stiff and helpless but not dangerously hurt, only grieving that I couldn't take the battery. I would have done it if they hadn't run it off and I would have had the earth work if I had 300 men instead of 20.

I don't murmur but I would be very grateful to God if I might have done it even though I hadn't come back from it, for no advance can be made without taking it. The force suffered a good deal all regiments losing officers especially Comm. Officers. Col. Hartwell of 55th Mass. is wounded, I hear Col. Lewis is also, but don't know certainly. We were about 4 miles from R Road, & could hear the guns coming with enforcements.

Then the Rebs would yell and howl.

Dec. 3d Can't learn much from the front. It is reported that the enemy have abandoned the battery.

I'm pretty blue and helpless but in less pain when quiet. The 54th & 55th undertook to charge the earth work and were driven back. That's what mixed them all up with my men. I am going to try to be sent to Jacksonville as soon as I can be moved. You had better remain until hearing again from me. Don't be worried dearest it will all come out right by and by. The surgeon is going to try for the ball in my right thigh today & will probably find it. At all events it will not do harm beyond limping now for a month or so. Give my love to Mrs. Willard. Say that the Lt. Col. is unhurt & is in command.

God bless my beloved wife.

I only know of Capt. White & Lt. Kolb wounded.

Lovingly your husband

J. C. Beecher

I can't hear anything from my "Kate" [his other horse] but hope she is alive & safe.[63]

*James Beecher.*

Colonel Beecher was wounded three times and hit again in the left hand, but fortunately the bullet was spent and did not do much damage. In an interesting aside, after the war, James met a colonel from the Confederate Army who also had fought in the battle of Honey Hill. The officer told him it was not by accident that he and his great gray horse were hit so many times: the word had been passed to the Rebel soldiers to aim at the officer on the light gray horse. Colonel Beecher's men carried his saddle from the battlefield and returned it to him when he was released from the hospital.

Another more gruesome account of the battle, one that appeared in a Confederate newspaper, the *Savannah Republican*, in December, reported:

> The Negroes, as usual, formed the advance, and had nearly reached the creek when our batteries opened upon them down the road with a terrible volley of special case. This threw them into temporary confusion, but the entire force, estimated at five thousand, was quickly restored to order, and thrown into a line of battle parallel with our own, up and down the margin of swamp. Thus the battle raged from eleven in the morning till dark. The enemy's centre and left were most exposed and suffered terribly. Their right was posted behind an old dam that ran through the swamp, and it maintained its position till the close of the fight. Our left was very much exposed, and an attempt was once or twice made by the enemy to turn it by advancing through the swamp and up the hill, but they were driven back without a prolonged struggle.
>
> The centre and left of the enemy fought with a desperate

earnestness. Several attempts were made to charge our batteries, and many got nearly across the swamp, but were in every instance forced back by the galling fire poured into them from our lines. We made a visit to the field the following day, and found the road literally strewn with their dead. Some eight or ten bodies were floating in the water where the road crosses, and in a ditch on the roadside just beyond we saw six Negroes piled one on top of the other. A colonel of one of the Negro regiments, with his horse, was killed while fearlessly leading his men across the creek in a charge. With that exception, all the dead and wounded officers were carried off by the enemy during the night.[64]

*Union Army field hospital.*

At the battle of Honey Hill, the Union had 750 casualties; Beecher's regiment lost 114 men, with only the 55th Massachusetts and the 25th Ohio losing more, 137 and 138, respectively. The Confederates had only 150 to 200 casualties.

Shortly after the battle, Lt. Col. A. J. Willard, who was in charge of the 35th U.S.C.T. regiment at Honey Hill wrote to his wife back in Jacksonville with Frances Beecher. Willard's wife notified her father of the battle and the wounding of Colonel Beecher and he in turn notified Henry Ward Beecher about his brother James:

New York, 34 Pine Street
Dec. 16, 1864
Rev. Henry Ward Beecher,

Dear Sir,

Knowing how anxious you must feel to hear from your brother (Col. B), I hasten to send you such information as has come to me—
My son in law A. J. Willard is his Lieut. Col.—and I received letters from my daughter yesterday, dated at Jacksonville, Fla., the 6th instant. She writes that orders came on the 25th ult. for some four or five Regiments there to leave immediately for Hilton Head—and they did leave accordingly on the 27th—Your brother had charge of the whole force as Brig. Gen.; and Willard took command of the Regt.—
For some ten days no steamer arrived at Jacksonville—Mrs. Beecher and Mrs. Willard the only ladies there—all the troops gone except the small force left garrison the fort—The chaplain the only one left behind to care for the ladies—They continued in ignorance of all that was transpiring until the

5th Dec—when a steamer arrived bringing intelligence of
the battle and skirmishes which had occurred—Colonel
Beecher was reported to have distinguished himself by his
bravery, and to have been <u>dangerously</u> wounded—But he
wrote to his wife that it was <u>not</u> so—It was true he had
received three distinct wounds (one in his left thigh) and
has been taken to the hospital at Beaufort, and requested his
wife to come immediately on to him—He wrote Mrs. B. that
the col. troops, and particularly his own Regiment behaved
nobly—never broke nor flinched—My daughter says your
brother is idolized by the men,—and that there is not a man
in the Regiment who would not sacrifice his life for him.
Mrs. Beecher was to leave Jacksonville on the 7th to join
her husband—

I am sir,

Yours Truly

Z. Platt[65]

# 12

*Marching toward Charleston,*
*Freeing Slaves, Zion Church*

After he recovered from his wounds, Colonel Beecher was discharged from the hospital at Christmas; when his health improved enough so that he could travel, he was given a furlough, and he and Frances traveled to the North. Upon his return, he again reported to Hilton Head and to General Hatch, who commanded the Coast Division of the Department of the South. On Saturday, February 18, he rejoined his regiment at Combahee Ferry on the Combahee River in South Carolina.

Colonel Beecher arrived at 10:00 A.M. and found every man in ranks, waiting. As he appeared before them, they cheered loudly, and he was touched by their enthusiasm. The officers all came over, and Colonel Beecher delightedly shook hands with everyone.

On Sunday, while waiting for rations, he held a service along with the 107th New York Infantry Regiment, and on Monday, he and his regiment marched at dawn and set out camping, raiding, and burning through South Carolina. At times he was in the saddle from 6:00 A.M. until 6:00 P.M., and he and the 35th U. S. Colored Troops continued their march to Charleston, freeing slaves and collecting contraband on the way, including chickens, oxen, and horses. No regular Rebel troops were encountered, but Colonel Beecher did meet a Methodist preacher from whom he took three horses. The preacher begged that he might keep the horses, but Colonel Beecher replied that "he and his brother ministers by their preaching, have forced one to leave the pulpit & taken to fighting and I'd not only take his horses but burn his house if it came in my line of march."[66]

*"Marching on! — The Fifty-Fifth Massachusetts Colored Regiment Singing John Brown's March in the Streets of Charleston, South Carolina, February 21, 1865."*

On a raid a week later, Colonel Beecher and a company

of his regiment arrived at the Limerick Plantation on the Cooper River in Berkeley County, South Carolina. On the plantation there lived 250 slaves who worked primarily in the rice fields, and they knew in advance that the black Union troops would be arriving. The plantation had been visited by other Union soldiers twice that day before the men of the 35th marched onto the front lawn, with Colonel Beecher riding at the head of the column. When the company was halted, his men, being former slaves, went straight to the barnyard, where they found the "call bell," a bell that was used to call the slaves to and from the fields. The men of the 35th removed the bell from its mountings and took great satisfaction in destroying it.

The plantation owner appeared at the front door of the large house to admit Colonel Beecher, who had only one demand, and that was that he wished to see everyone on the front lawn. There was a mixture of apprehension and fear among the slaves after they had assembled. However, the colonel, who had joined the Union army and set aside his Bible for a sword because he strongly believed in the abolition of slavery, must have experienced personal satisfaction when he stated to the hundreds of slaves that had gathered: "You are free as birds, you don't have to work for these people anymore!"[67] Many sang and danced, others dropped to their knees and prayed.

Later in the day, Colonel Beecher was relaxing in the yard with the plantation owner, who then called Maum Hetty, an elderly slave woman, for table service. Colonel Beecher refused the service, saying she was no longer a slave, and each time the owner called Maum Hetty to bring something, Colonel Beecher refused to allow her to serve him, even a pitcher of water, telling the owner "that Hetty was no longer a slave, and therefore she could not be bossed."[68]

*Zion Church at 123 Calhoun Street, Charleston, South Carolina.*

Colonel Beecher's 35th U. S. Colored Troops had such a high reputation for discipline and efficiency that the unit was kept in the service after the war and participated in special duty around Charleston as an army of occupation. On March 12, 1865, Colonel Beecher celebrated the capture of the city by preaching at the largest church in the city, Zion Church, on Calhoun Street. The people of Charleston must have heard that a Beecher was going to be preaching—the church, which easily seated 1,500, was attended by both black and white citizens. Captain Henry O. Marcy, a regimental surgeon who was present that day, wrote of Beecher:

> He entered the pulpit in full uniform, through a crowd that filled every standing place, followed by members of his staff. Unbuckling his sword and laying it tenderly on the desk, he took for his text, "The Liberty wherewith Christ hath made us free." His impassioned oratory at times swayed the vast

audience, as a mighty wind the tree-tops; again, recounting God's care for his children, it fell as the soft dews from heaven, and there was not a dry eye in the house; and when at the close all bent in prayer, broken sobs and utterances of, "Thanks to God we's free" attested his power.[69]

Colonel Beecher went on to preach at Zion Church as long as he was stationed in Charleston.

# 13

*The Freedmen's Bureau*

At the beginning of April, Colonel Beecher was promoted to brevet brigadier general, and he became a Freedmen's Bureau subassistant commissioner in charge of the northern half of Charleston, ninety square miles that included more than 600 plantations, two large towns, and the sea islands.

The Freedmen's Bureau was established by Congress in March of 1865 and was aimed at protecting former slaves' freedoms and integrating them into Southern culture and society as American citizens and laborers. The United States Civil War officially ended May 9, 1865. Approximately four million slaves were freed following the Union Army's victory, communities were in ruins, and the plantation economy was destroyed.

General Beecher was one of many members of the Freedmen's Bureau who faced the difficult job of reconstruction among the white population, assisting the former slaves to understand their new responsibilities, and establishing work contracts between the now free people and the planters. The Freedmen's Bureau duties also included providing food, shelter, and medical and legal assistance, establishing schools, and settling former slaves on Confederate lands that were abandoned or confiscated during the war.

Of this time in their life together, Frances Beecher would reminisce in an article written years later:

> Our Sunday services... were frequently held in the groves, which were God's first temples. The General found that the freed people, being religiously inclined, could be taught their new duties in no way so well as by his plain sermons and speeches, combined with singing and prayer. Therefore many a romantic and beautiful spot, where country roads intersected, saw a quiet Sunday crowd, sitting on fallen trees, fence rails, stones, and even on horseback and in wagons, listening to the eloquent teacher with eager attention. Men, white and black, with women and little children were there; and at the close what hand-shakings and blessings there were! My memory pictures of those scenes I value most of all.[70]

General Beecher had been an able commander, admired by his men, and a compassionate administrator under difficult circumstances; needless to say, the Freedmen's Bureau was unpopular with Southerners, who despised having to deal with black Federal soldiers. However, General Beecher was a skilled negotiator, and he developed good rapports between the former slaves, planters, and plantation owners in the occupied South. Planters believed one of

the reasons for Beecher's success in settling disputes was his ability
to work with the men who had been slaves. He was said to have
had a good working relationship with his officers and troops, as
well as with the Southern planters. One newspaper claimed that
he was "honest, bold, uncompromising and consistent, with his
whole heart in the work of securing equal rights to all men without
regard to color, he has brought order out of confusion and obtained
the confidence of both the freedmen and their late owners."[71]

*Veterans of the Civil War.*

In September of 1865, General Beecher wrote to a friend
of his frustrations with General John P. Hatch, who was the
commander of the occupied forces in Charleston and who had

headed the expeditionary force at the battle of Honey Hill. He believed General Hatch had prejudices towards black troops, and Beecher was growing more restless every day. He would have resigned, except that he loved his men and knew they needed him.

In November, the commanding general, Quincy A. Gillmore, ordered that rations distributed by the Freedmen's Bureau should be distributed only to "freed people" and not to impoverished whites. General Beecher looked upon this decision as unfair and believed that if whites could not receive rations, neither should blacks. General Beecher was joined in his opposition to this policy by General Rufus Saxton and General Charles Devens, Jr., and together they tried to get rations for whites. Beecher wrote that "to turn [white women and children] away & pick out black faces, is simply to do the very thing we are trying not to do, i.e., increase antipathy between whites and blacks, and establish a color test."[72]

In time, because of a shortage of personnel and funding, the bureau had difficulty fulfilling its goals, and the goodwill accomplished by General Beecher and his soldiers ceased. After participating in the affairs of Reconstruction in the military district of Charleston, the 35th U.S.C.T. was mustered out of the service when their three-year enlistments ended on June 1, 1866. The regiment assembled, and each soldier was quietly discharged from the United States Army. Several of the men wrote Frances Beecher expressing their love for General Beecher, thanking both of them for their devotion. The regiment, during its three years of active duty, had served its country well, and the men took home a greater sense of self-worth that changed many for the rest of their lives.

James Beecher's military career lasted five turbulent years; he had joined in June of 1861, when he was thirty-three years of age, and stayed in the army for an extended period after the Civil

War was over. A few years later at a reunion dinner held by the officers of the 35th U.S.C.T. Regiment in Worcester, Massachusetts, Major James N. Croft made a brief address, "concluding with this sentiment, which was greeted with applause: 'Our brave Beecher distinguished as a preacher, as a sailor, and not less as a soldier."[73]

Years later, the men of the 35th U.S.C.T. requested from Frances Beecher a life-size portrait of their "beloved" Colonel. In 1887, Post #22 of the Grand Army of the Republic was formed in New Bern, North Carolina, and was named the James C. Beecher Post, a "touching memorial" to a "faithful" Northern officer who taught them to be men.

Throughout his life, James Beecher had little patience for conditions he viewed as unjust; in the army it was difficult for him to understand why officers did not act more quickly to deal with a situation instead of following army protocol, which often left things hanging or worked so slowly that he found it unbearable. He was a man of action, and in his mind, following all the rules and regulations to the letter often delayed what was obvious. He also deplored political decisions taking precedence over what he saw was either right or wrong.

# 14

A *Return to the Pulpit—or Maybe Not:*
*Seeking Trout, and Finding Bliss*

After the Civil War, James Beecher returned to the church and temporarily took over his brother Thomas's church at Elmira, New York. In May of 1867, he became the pastor of the Owego Congregational Church in Owego, New York. While at Owego, he and his wife Frances built a home and became part of the community. The Beechers stayed for four years, with James preaching his last sermon on March 19, 1871. He then took a position with the Congregational Church of Poughkeepsie, New York. The church had a long history of its members being involved in the antislavery movement: the abolitionist Frederick Douglass spoke before the church's congregation as early as 1847.

During his years at the Congregational Church of Pough-keepsie, the Reverend James Beecher was at times compared in his eloquence as an orator to his brother, Henry Ward Beecher.[74] James would on occasion substitute for the eminent Henry Ward and occupy the pulpit of the celebrated Plymouth Church in Brooklyn. In August of 1871, he officiated for his brother while Henry was on vacation. While there, James also conducted two evening lectures on China before large crowds, recalling his experiences and the culture of the Chinese people. He also made a plea to his audience to welcome Chinese immigrants to America and to treat them with kindness.

*Plymouth Church in Brooklyn, New York.*

In both Owego and Poughkeepsie, the Reverend Beecher was known for taking a keen interest in his parishioners, and he and Frances formed close relationships with many. Friends recalled that during this time James tended to "undervalue his work and his worth."[75] While at Poughkeepsie, the Beechers were visited by James's sister Isabella in 1873. She found that he was well liked by his congregation, but he seemed depressed, and their home seemed gloomy, even though he and Frances had adopted a baby daughter. Isabella was not really concerned about James's mood, for she had often seen the same mental attitude in her brother Thomas, who had experienced throughout his life "fits of despondency."[76]

It was a year after Isabella's visit to Poughkeepsie that James visited the Willewemoc Club at Sand Pond, in Ulster County. Several members of the club resided in Poughkeepsie, and during the trouting season of 1874, they invited Reverend Beecher to spend his vacation at their clubhouse and enjoy the trout fishing.

James Beecher deeply appreciated the natural world, and he usually spent his vacations fishing and camping, often in the most secluded parts of the country. He was joined at Sand Pond by his brother, Reverend Thomas K. Beecher. While at Sand Pond, the brothers decided to explore the surrounding mountains of the primitive region and took off from the lodge with their knapsacks and fishing tackle. They both enjoyed being outdoors, especially the adventures that go along with exploring unknown forest lands and the excitement of fishing unfamiliar and remote trout streams.

They headed northerly through the woods, up steep mountainsides and over ridges, around rock ledges, and down through a forest of hardwoods that contained beech, birch, maple, ash, and occasional stands of hemlock. They were in an area that was south of Mill Brook Ridge and west of Balsam Lake Mountain and was known on early maps as "Big Woods."

The average elevation was about 3,200 feet, with each mountain being so close in height to the others that there was not much of a view to guide them. Because their hike was not along a charted course, it was more to their liking; but when they found a cold mountain stream, they followed it down until they reached the storied Beaverkill. The brothers fished their way up the Beaverkill and came to a tributary that looked inviting, then traveled northerly along the stream until they came to a lake.

At the end of a tiring and lengthy hike, the lovely lake that the Beechers discovered was encircled by mountains with densely wooded peaks that formed a large amphitheater. It was approximately 20 acres in size and was known to locals as Thomas Lake, though it did not appear on the Brink & Tillson map of 1854, nor J. H. French's popular survey map of 1858.[77] The latter map did show an unnamed lake, the outflow stream of which entered the

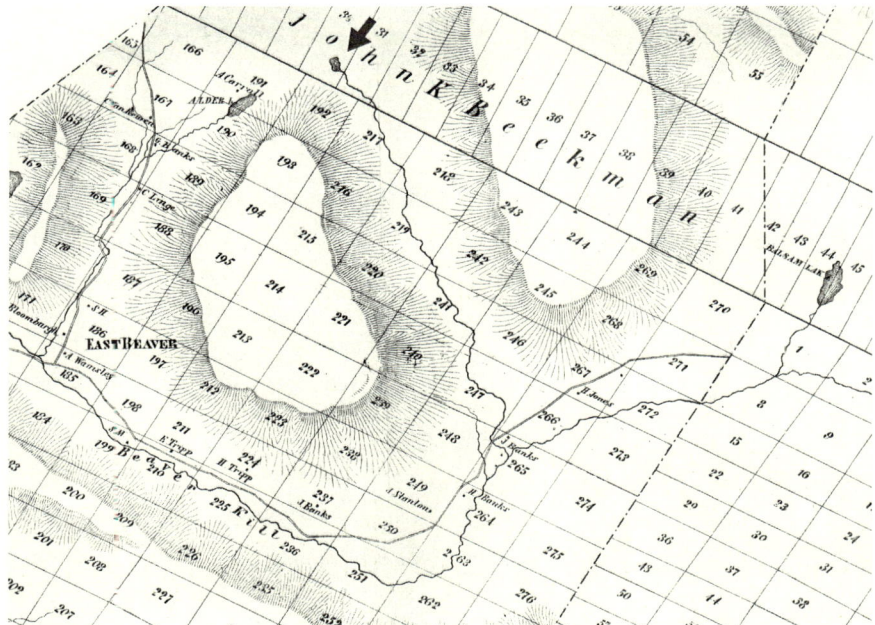

*J. H. French 1858 survey of Ulster County, NY, showing incorrect location of Beecher Lake.*

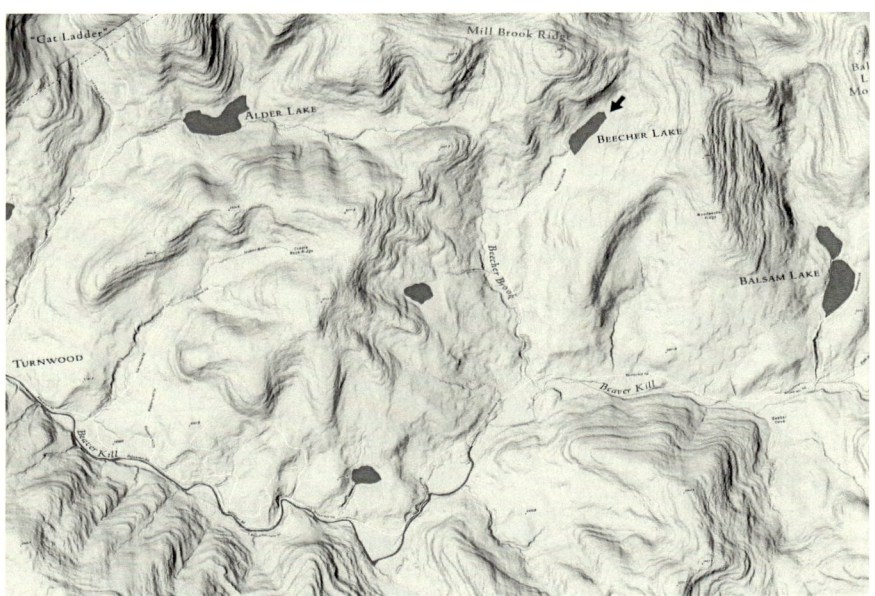

*Modern map of Ulster County, NY based on USGS data, showing correct location of Beecher Lake.*

Beaverkill where Beecher Brook enters today; but the unnamed lake was miles from where Thomas Lake is located, and the lake shown on French's survey map did not exist. It is easy to understand why James believed he had the right to name the unknown body of water Beecher Lake. In fact, even when the name was accepted and placed on the Beer's Atlas of 1875, the location on the Beer's map was still far from its true location.[78]

The lake was unspoiled; its waters were clear and cold, contained fine trout, and offered choice fishing. The brothers camped along its shores, and James stayed for six weeks, subsisting by hunting and fishing.

When James Beecher stood on the shore, he was awed by the peacefulness of the pristine surroundings. He thought it was the perfect retreat; a place of bliss that was exactly what he had been searching for, a primitive forest where he could commune with nature amidst picturesque scenery and solitude.

While Thomas was a skilled fly fisher and fine shot, he opted to stay in camp, cooking, washing dishes, drying clothes, and making fires. James had been assigned the job of bringing in the trout, shooting partridges, and gathering food for the table. The nearest store for any type of supplies was ten miles away, and a blazed path guided them back and forth through the forest.

Thomas was also an accomplished writer, and in the fall, he wrote of their experience in the September 9 issue of the *Christian Union* in an article titled "In the Woods." His story was a reminiscence of the adventure and of the gratification the brothers encountered along the headwaters of the Beaverkill and the lake. He did not name the location where they camped, other than to say that he and James were conveniently located on the shore of a fine trout lake so isolated that there were probably no more than a

*Beecher Lake.* Lee Van Put

dozen people for miles. He also wrote that they had brought little
into the woods and had to hunt and fish to supplement their meals.

> …our little lake, which at this hour—sunset—is no longer
> water, but a duplication of sky and glorified mountain.
> Nature lavishes beauty on these nameless little mountain
> ponds as prodigally as upon the famous lakes which tourists
> cross the seas to visit. We are high above sea level. Hardy
> birches and beeches, with running roots three and four rods
> long, cling to the outcropping stones, and make tall slender
> growth through the year that frosts them in every month. I
> trace their stems in the lake, and could draw the mountain
> as accurately from its reflection as from direct vision.[79]

Thomas ends his article by writing: "Four weeks in the
woods. Never mind where. Trout, and what is more, appetite
every day, and sleep every night, with moon and stars at their best;
weather most lady-like, weeping rarely and for good purposes."[80]

Believing they were the first to discover the lake, James
Beecher decided he had the right to name it Beecher Lake. He was
so captivated by his environment, its serenity, and the beautiful
region of the Beaverkill Valley that the forty-six-year-old preacher
decided to abandon the comforts of city life and relocate in what
at the time was considered a virgin wilderness.

# 15

## Beecher Lake

Upon returning to the city of Poughkeepsie and civilization, James learned the lake and its surrounding lands were owned by James S. Van Cleef of the same city. He purchased Beecher Lake and lot 38 of Great Lot 9 and approximately 150 acres from Van Cleef on September 28, 1874, and during the winter, he decided to leave the church in Poughkeepsie. In transferring the title to Beecher, Van Cleef reserved to himself and members of the Willewemoc Club a right-of-way to and from the lake and the right to fish its waters. The following spring, the Reverend James Beecher resigned his pastorate and decided to live with his family along the upper Beaverkill at Beecher Lake.

Many were surprised that he resigned from the Congregational Church of Poughkeepsie, where he was extremely popular, had a flourishing parish, an annual salary of $3,000, and six weeks' vacation. James told a magazine reporter that he did not tire of civilization, but loved his mountain retreat more. He preached his farewell sermon on April 28, 1875.

That summer, James and Thomas again fished the Beaver-kill, camped along its banks, and vacationed on the shore of Beecher Lake. The nearest post office was about seven miles from Beecher Lake, at Turnwood, which was identified as "East Beaver" on the 1858 survey map of J. H. French.

At the lake, James first erected a fly tent and then a wall or hospital-style tent with a board floor and an opening in the back to admit heat from a wood stove on cold days. This tent was erected near a spring that flowed into the lake. He also constructed a crude cottage or shanty, which had a dining and cooking room, with open sides facing the lake, where he cleared some land.

Frances Beecher was forty-three years old when she joined her husband at Beecher Lake. A graduate of Mount Holyoke College in 1851 and a fine writer, years later she would reminisce about the dining facility, writing that better food was never eaten nor enjoyed more than what was consumed in the shanty, and that the mountain air procreated an appetite for simple food. In an article titled "A Seven Years' Outing" published in *New England Magazine*, she wrote:

> But the veriest gourmand could have asked no better breakfast than was furnished by those delicate trout, only half an hour from the pure water of the lake, half a pound in weight and dotted with the most brilliant colors, which neither oven nor frying pan could change. These trout, baked in cream and served with the best of corn muffins and coffee, and discussed in the open air with one of Nature's loveliest

pictures in full view, might well elevate the prosaic business of eating into a fine art.[81]

James would eventually add two more lots to his holdings, totaling 300 acres. It was said that James Beecher could swing a woodsman's axe as easily as he could cast a fly over the smooth waters of Beecher Lake, and he began working on a trail to bring in materials to construct a year-round residence. At first, there was just a wide path cut through the forest that at times went around mountains that were too rough or too difficult to go over. The path or trail forded small streams, and where larger ones needed to be crossed, small bridges of logs were constructed.

The nearest settlement with a sawmill was more than nine miles away, at Shin Creek (Lew Beach), and to get the lumber to the lake, the trail through the forest needed to be widened into a road. Beecher's neighbors, though few and far between, some ten miles distant, got together and helped Reverend Beecher construct a wagon road from the lake to the post office in Turnwood. In return, James furnished and placed windows and doors, and made other improvements to their simple log cabins. He did a great amount of good and was kind to the poor, giving freely to the point where he himself was "poor of purse."

Once the lumber was secured, James, a skilled carpenter, built a one-and-a-half story wood-framed house entirely by himself, completing the work just before winter. The building, said to have been constructed in the finest manner, had a huge fireplace, a large bay window, and a fine veranda that faced the lake. Beecher, being a trout fisherman, was entertained daily watching the gentle rises and circular swirls made by the abundant brook trout as they fed on the surface of the beautiful lake.

*The house at Beecher Lake.*

Though married at the time, James decided to spend that first winter at the lake alone. He had no nearby neighbors, and in this secluded region with no companionship, there was only solitude, and the sounds of winter storms, and the nighttime screech of wildcats and mountain lions. His wife and adopted daughter came to the lake in the spring of 1875. Until then, Frances Beecher was a faithful correspondent, writing often. The mail from the post office at Turnwood arrived only once a week, and to receive her letters, James would have to trek fourteen miles round trip, on foot, through drifting snow and freezing temperatures.

When the Beechers settled at the lake, the region was still considered a primitive wilderness, one of the least-settled areas of New York State. Wildlife was abundant, and the few inhabitants who lived in the valley were backwoodsmen who inhabited log cabins and subsisted by hunting and fishing. Up until this time, the region's visitors were outdoorsmen, mostly trout fishermen; some, members of the Willewemoc Club who hiked over the mountains from their clubhouse at Sand Pond to fish the Beaverkill and Balsam Lake. Other trout fishing tourists found their way up the Beaverkill and boarded at Weaver's, Leal's, Tripp's, or Walmsley's, or at the famous resort of James and Hannah Murdock, just upstream of Shin Creek.

The mail arrived every Friday, and the route ran from Morsston (Livingston Manor) on the New York & Oswego Midland Railroad to Margaretville on the Ulster & Delaware Railroad. Those inhabitants living along the upper Beaverkill at the time liked to tell the tale of how they, through great perseverance, influenced the postal department to establish the route along primitive trails through the forest. The residents wanted the service so badly they agreed to carry the mail for $300 per year. The route ran over mountains so precipitous one was called the "cat ladder," and it was reported that "men make their way over it with hands and feet, but there has been found a horse that does manage to crawl over it with the bag tightly strapped upon his back."[82]

About this time, a man from Illinois bid on all the routes, including the one from Livingston Manor to Margaretville. Bidding at a lower price, he received the new contract, though after acquiring the route he immediately began writing letters to the people around Turnwood, hoping they would take it off his hands. The story that circulated at the time was that the local people wanted the "prairie mail carrier" to have a go at going over the "cat ladder" and that he would "doubtless be greatly astonished when he undertakes it."[83]

*Delivering the mail in winter.*

# 16

---

*James Preaches, Frances Teaches*

Shortly after the Beechers moved to the lake, their few and scattered neighbors visited them and asked James to preach at the
nearest one-room schoolhouse, which was about four miles away.
He agreed and alternated preaching between the schoolhouse near
Beecher Lake and another farther down the Beaverkill near the
base of Touchmenot Mountain, about two miles upstream of Shin
Creek, now on the property of Joan Wulff and the Wulff School of
Fly Fishing. The "mountaineers" turned out each Sunday in summer
to listen to his sermons, and when he preached a sermon near Shin
Creek, the scattered settlers traveled miles to hear this Beecher of
the forest, whom they learned to love and respect.

He received no pay and refused to accept any. One Sunday,
in July 1877, while preaching at the schoolhouse upstream of Lew
Beach, about ten miles from his home, the congregation offered to

take up a collection to compensate him. But he positively refused to let this happen, halting the idea with a few words and adding that if people were willing to come to hear the Gospel, his services should be free. On this occasion, Reverend Beecher had provided a parlor organ for the service, which was attended by more than the usual crowd and included summer boarders and fishermen from New York. The Reverend Beecher administered the entire service himself: he played the organ, led the singing, and preached the sermon. The residents along the Beaverkill believed that Rev. Beecher retired from regular preaching because he was tired of "doctrinal forms and the perpetual jarring of the sects."[84]

In the audience this day was a correspondent from the *Hartford Weekly Times*, who wrote an article titled "Trout Fishing in the Woods." The author was a trout fisherman who traveled to the Beaverkill over rough mountain roads in a buckboard, a ride he described as unbearable and dangerous. He cited the region as being famous for its trout fishing and wrote that most of the residents were either "lumbermen" or "bark-peelers" for the tannery at Beaverkill. He also reported that the moment Reverend Beecher began preaching, it was obvious he was a "genuine Beecher through and through."[85] The correspondent wrote that one of Beecher's first remarks was that he understood theology when he left college, but does not know anything about it now, and he recalled that—like a great many other preachers—Beecher began teaching people things he did not really know himself.

The correspondent reported that his sermon was unpretentious and contained amusing anecdotes throughout that had his audience laughing quietly. Beecher's unconventional style reminded several visitors of Henry Ward Beecher's eccentricities at Plymouth Church in Brooklyn. The correspondent also wrote that James had a quaint, quiet manner and a large supply of humorous stories he used freely when preaching. Beecher spoke with a matter-of-fact style and related to his audience some of the problems he was having with his cow. The cow was allowed to browse in the woods because Beecher had no pasture, and she wandered all day. In the evening, he had to hunt for her, while she made it a point to get as far away from the house as she could. "If she gets a glimpse of him hunting around for her, where she thinks he can't see her" the correspondent writes,

> she stands stock still and looks at him. She'll stand there, said Mr. Beecher, and look, and look, and look, hoping all the time I don't see her, and all the flies on the Beaverkill couldn't make her swing her tail, lest the motion should make her ring the bell on her neck. When at last he gets up to her and shoos her toward home, off she goes as gentle as a lamb, and then he wonders why she couldn't do that just as well without bringing him away out there and then playing hide and seek through the woods.[86]

Subsisting along the upper Beaverkill Valley was difficult; residents eked out a living on soil that was poor, steep, and stony, in an area where frosts could occur during any month of the year. Although rain was abundant, crops other than forage grasses used for pasture, grazing, and hay were difficult to grow, and to borrow a phrase from the naturalist John Burroughs, people there "lived close to the bone." The Beechers recognized their neighbors' needs and were generous with their time, support, and financial and personal resources.

According to Frances, as time went on, these Sunday

gatherings became very important to the men, women, children, and entire families who came from near and far. The services were looked upon as a treat or a special event, one that brought these isolated people together to picnic, socialize, and receive religious teachings. They came by buckboard or by horseback down roads or trails into the valley or through the woods on foot. The Beaverkill people soon desired to improve their singing abilities, which encouraged a "singing school" taught by the Reverend Beecher, who provided an organ and blackboard.

This led to improving the public schools, which were in session for only six months of the year. Many children and young men were unable to read or write, others not able to read a book aloud comfortably; a situation that Frances Beecher found appalling and began to correct by taking over the teaching duties personally, after applying for the position of public school teacher. Within three months, Frances had students writing letters and had a young man of twenty-five years of age learning to read and write in two weeks' time. City friends of the Beechers began sending writing tablets, desks, and books.

Frances Beecher began teaching at the nearest school (today it still stands opposite the Salmo Fontinalis Club) and introduced books to families that had never known them before. She received $60 each year for her teaching duties, and she combined this amount with $75 to $100 more of her own money and bought clothing and books for the needy "backwoods children."

After the completion of the road from Beecher Lake to Turnwood, James purchased a horse that Frances would hitch to a wagon every Friday to get the mail in Turnwood. The wagon was a gift from friends of the Congregational Church in Poughkeepsie and was made to order, said to be "the longest and safest buckboard ever made,"[87] The seat was on top of a wide, but low pyramidal storage box that was spacious and was used for hauling supplies to the lake. When the horse was not hitched to the wagon, James used it and his old army saddle to travel by horseback.

*The schoolhouse in Hardenburgh.* ED VAN PUT

One county official recalled that "Mr. Beecher was always ready to do a good deed, and that he visited the people, gave money and the necessities of life."[88] He recalled that he had known Reverend Beecher to get up in the middle of the night and ride his horse to Margaretville, a distance of twenty-five miles, to get a doctor for a neighbor.

At Christmas, the school became the center of attention. Frances decorated the one-room building as it had never been done before, with evergreen boughs and a Christmas tree trimmed with fruits from the city that delighted young and old. In winter, travel was easier and more pleasant; the snow was generally deep enough to become solid when packed by teams with sleds, creating good roads to move around on.

Sleighing was a joyful way to move about, and having less work at this time of year encouraged these early inhabitants to visit one another, creating a social life they found most enjoyable. It was common for an entire family to be loaded into a large wooden sled that was pulled with oxen, or into a box sleigh filled with hay or straw and drawn by a pair of horses, and make an all-day visit to a neighbor who lived at quite a distance. The visitors were welcomed, and hospitality flourished. A jar of buckwheat batter was always ready for company and "thick, white, fluffy griddle cakes and maple syrup, such as city folks know nothing about" were served at any time of the day. "Lifelong friendships were formed between the pastor and his family and the people, and generosity and good feeling flourished."[89]

*An ox-drawn box sleigh.*

The Beechers were a part of this winter social life of the upper Beaverkill Valley, and had many winter visitors at Beecher

Lake from their scattered neighbors. Recalling these times and of her wonderful years spent at the lake, Frances Beecher reminisced:

> The talk was friendly and pleasant, as there was little sickness to discuss or worries and jealousies and rivalries to bring forward. Kindly feeling prevailed. Yet these people lived in such houses that they often had to construct a spare room by a festoon of bedquilts, and you would have said they were to be pitied for their poverty. Not at all! "Happiness, like heaven, does not depend upon situation," nor on the abundance of things a man hath.[90]

# 17

## *Life in the Forest*

During their years at the lake, the Beechers adopted infant twin daughters; along with their older sister, the children made pets or playmates of the squirrels and chipmunks, and the Beechers raised domestic ducks and chickens. They familiarized themselves with the abundant wildlife in the area, and to supplement their food supply they occasionally added wild game to their menu. On occasion, neighbors invited them to a dinner of bear meat, which Frances found to be the most delicious meat they had ever tasted, with the twins asking for seconds.

While deer were not plentiful around the lake, they were hunted, and when success was achieved, they provided memorable meals of roasted venison. The Beechers' table was at times supplied with woodchucks or wild ducks and pigeons that were flying south in the fall or early winter. Rabbits were common, and were hunted after the first snow, furnishing a "savory stew, roast or pie.' Roast goose was also an option, because at least one valley resident raised geese and provided them for special occasions. But their favorite bird was partridge or grouse, which were abundant and considered a delicacy.

*"View from Beecher's Bay Window."*

Trout were a family staple, their savor perhaps enhanced because of the challenge of catching them. Frances recalled how beautiful the lake was with the first cool autumn sunsets, when trout would rise all across the lake, leaping out of the water in every direction in their pursuit of hatching caddis or mayflies. At these times Frances exhibited her fly-fishing skills by tying a fly to her leader and taking a boat, with someone to steady it, to those places she intended to cast her Coachman, Claret Gnat, or Beaverkill wet fly into the swirls left by rising trout. In twenty minutes of fishing, she usually caught enough trout to furnish her family with their favorite breakfast.

One of the most anticipated times of the year was "sap season," when spiles were placed in maple trees and pails were hung below them to catch the sap. When the sap was collected, sugar making began by boiling the clear liquid, converting maple sap to syrup by the removal of water and "sugaring off" into cakes. Cakes were made in every conceivable shape, and most families participated in the process—children, too, enjoyed sugar making, tasting and sampling the almost-finished products. Both James and Frances worked each spring when the snow began melting. When the weather was good, they worked day and night boiling the sap at the sugar camp. After the sap stopped flowing, the snow disappeared, and the search for wildflowers would begin.

Frances Beecher had an affinity for the abundant wild berries that were found throughout the Beaverkill Valley. She believed that wild strawberries, though smaller than domestically raised ones, have a more pleasant, savory smell, a sweeter flavor, and are therefore tastier. Wild raspberry season followed the strawberries, and that meant canning and making jelly. Frances's thoughts on raspberries were somewhat similar: she agreed that cultivation might make them larger, but the berries then lost their "characteristic flavor," and to taste these berries "in their perfection," they should be eaten, like trout, in their natural habitat.

She greatly enjoyed living at Beecher Lake. Life was simple and uncomplicated, and she strongly believed that it was the best place to raise their children. She lived in a natural world where worries were few and the larger decisions that affected their lives were often decided by weather or natural events. Nature provided many of the wants and needs of the family, such as comfort, food, shelter, pleasure, and the necessities of everyday living. The Beechers possessed a kindness that was not found in most people, and Frances and her husband were happiest when helping others. Not only were they generous with their time, labor, and the small finances they managed, they tried to encourage their neighbors to help one another, as well.

Frances loved the changes that each season brought; hardship was something she never experienced because her mindset was positive, and she saw goodness in the natural world. One of her favorite times of the year was autumn, when nature provides those exquisite scenes found only in the Catskills; scenes that were captured in the landscapes of the artists of the Hudson River School.

She revered the beauty of the forest, whose stately beeches, birches, maples, and hemlocks ran from the shores of the lake to the highest summits of the mountains. Their fall foliage was filled with dazzling colors, brilliant reds and oranges, bright yellows and greens. She was filled with wonder at how these colors were duplicated on the mirrored surface of the lake in such exactness that one could not be sure if one were seeing the reflection or the tree itself. When reminiscing about these times years later she writes: "These days were softly lived, one hardly knowing whether one were in heaven or on earth."[91]

The Beechers referred to their retreat as "lakeside," and being part of a famous family and living in such a picturesque location, they were visited, primarily in summer, by friends and family. Newspaper reports wrote of visits by Harriet Beecher Stowe and Henry Ward Beecher, who camped and pitched tents at nearby Quaker Clearing and fished for trout while visiting James and his family.

Many found it difficult to comprehend how a man as educated and worldly as James Beecher would leave city life, give up a well-paying ministry with a flourishing congregation, move his family to the depths of a primitive forest that was barely settled, and toil and labor in such an environment. However, James Beecher had lived an extraordinary life, and perhaps he had found what he had long been seeking: a peaceful environment in a serene setting, away from the bustle, anxiety, and stress of everyday city life. He was not a selfish recluse, but ready to lend a helpful hand to those in need.

The Civil War had been over but a short time, and many veterans who served in this devastating conflict had difficulty putting the war behind them. James Beecher may also have had a similar problem. He was an exceptional soldier with an extraordinary military career, and he had experienced violent battlefield encounters. He had spent five years in a war in which he was responsible for the safety and welfare of men under his command whom he loved and whom he worried about every day. These experiences may have been one reason he chose to change his life and mend his psyche, enjoying a happy and peaceful life in a simple environment. That he chose an area so remote is not surprising. He loved the outdoors, and he was a trout fisherman. Many who fish for trout seek the solitude that can be found only in their natural settings; trout live in beautiful, unspoiled places, mainly in streams, rivers, lakes, and ponds with cold, clean water.

James extended the dimensions of their lakeside retreat and continued to clear the land of brush and trees, eventually securing about twenty acres under cultivation, where he grew buckwheat, oats, and hay. For his wayward cow, he constructed a barn made with logs. Eventually, the herd increased to three cows, and a butter-making facility was established. He deepened a cold spring and erected a springhouse and a churn over its icy waters. Jars of milk and cream were stored in its refrigerated interior.

James Beecher's brother Thomas and his family visited the lake every summer for six to eight weeks, during which the brothers, who enjoyed each other's company, would fish for trout and hunt grouse. An anecdotal story is told about Thomas, who in addition to being considered a man of great intellect and originality, was an ardent Beaverkill fly fisherman. It was said that he used primarily one fly pattern almost to the exclusion of all others, and on one occasion, a friend presented Thomas with a perfectly tied example of his favorite fly. Thomas immediately took the fly, dropped it on the ground, and trampled it before tying it on his leader. "Pardon me,' said Dr. Beecher. 'It was far and away too perfect. My trout are somewhat like the devil. They are suspicious and will not come near real excellence.'"[92]

While the Reverend James Beecher withdrew to a more quiet and restful existence, the fact that he was a Beecher still placed him in the news across the country. And though he had received several "flattering" offers to return to the pulpit, he did not intend to take up village or city life again.

To be a Beecher during his lifetime was particularly challenging. There was great pressure to live up to a public image that portrayed the Beechers as a family of prominent religious figures deeply involved in their faith, education, abolition, and literature.

"Beecher's Clearing."

Across America, family members were known for their forceful opinions and strong support for issues involving civil rights, women's rights, and social reform. Their thoughts and what they said or wrote in sermons and orations influenced a great many Americans, and newspapers and magazines reported on their activities. While Harriet Beecher Stowe is arguably the most well-known today, Henry Ward Beecher was the most celebrated in his time, and his preaching was said to be original and logical. He became a champion of abolition, preaching and writing that slavery is a sin.

While living at Beecher Lake, James did, on occasion, leave and preach at Plymouth Church in Brooklyn, filling in for his brother Henry. Plymouth Church had a seating capacity of 2,500 and the largest pipe organ in the United States. One newspaper carried a story in the spring of 1878 about a time when James occupied the pulpit of Plymouth Church. Looking around the extensive facility and its huge choir, large organ, and many ushers, James said, "I preach at home in a little schoolhouse in the wilderness. We have a little cabinet organ and I play it myself, because we have no organist. I am also sexton and usher. I play simple tunes to the glory of God and the rough backwoods people join in singing the hymns. I don't know anything about hell but I know a great deal about heaven."[93]

# 18

*"A Beecher in the Forest"*

No Beecher could escape the public eye for long, even when going off and living quietly, deep in the forest away from traveled roads. Shortly after James Beecher left the pulpit and retired to Beecher Lake, newspapers and magazine articles began appearing across the country with titles such as "A Beecher in Solitude," "A Preacher's Hermitage," "Beecher's Clearing," and "A Beecher in the Forest," describing how the Reverend James Beecher left civilization and wished to spend his remaining days and reporting that a Beecher was turning his back on urban life and had chosen instead to live a simple life not filled with obligations. Some believed his spirit or mental well-being was broken and that he was just in need of rest.

One of the first newspaper articles published about Beecher's decision to leave the Poughkeepsie Congregational Church and resettle at Beecher Lake was published in the *Middletown Press* in the summer of 1877, subtitled "The Attractions of the Beaverkill That Robbed Poughkeepsie of a Pastor." The newspaper reported that James Beecher was a lover of nature—the more primitive the forest the better—and that trout fishing the Beaverkill had brought him to the shores of the mountaintop lake. Here, it was written, he had found his ideal retreat, and remained for six weeks, enjoying the abundance of brook trout that inhabited Beecher Lake.

James described his first winter at the lake to a correspondent of the *New York World* and stated: "The stillness is profound; it seems to be something more than mere absence of sound; its negative character appears to give place to a positive, and the silence can absolutely be felt." The correspondent commented: "In this solitude Mr. Beecher is perfectly content; says he has never been satisfied before, and cannot be tempted out of it, and he expects to spend his days by the shores of his beautiful lake."[94]

One of the most popular articles, "Beecher's Clearing," was written by David W. Judd and appeared in the *American Agriculturist*, a monthly magazine, in September of 1881. Judd visited the lake and met with James and his brother Thomas. His article includes fine illustrations of the lake retreat and the homestead constructed by James, upon whom Judd bestowed the epithet "the hermit preacher." In Judd's interview, James is quoted as saying,

> A sailor by nature, and a minister by grace, I love to sit here by the hour, and look out upon these surroundings. They are a source of never-ending enjoyment. During the winter months I am still more fond of this retreat, for as the beautiful snow lies so still and quietly all about us, there is nothing to either disturb or discolor it. Here is true repose, and communion with nature.[95]

Most of the articles questioned why this Beecher chose to live in solitude. And they referred to James as a hermit, or an eccentric, and were critical of his lifestyle, even referring to him as having voluntarily exiled himself from civilization. However, one writer reported that James had not tired of civilization, but loved the tranquility of his mountain retreat more. Another, a correspondent from the *Brooklyn Daily Eagle*, saw things similarly; Henry Kimball wrote that "Mr. Beecher" was genial and "has not turned his back upon the world":

> We see no mystery or riddle to solve in order to justify him in his retirement. He has hosts of friends; they visit him from all parts of the land, and though Mrs. Beecher—the better half—says they do not keep a hotel, yet no good looking man or woman is allowed to pass Mr. Beecher's lake without breaking a corn dodger [a cake of cornbread] with him. His pork barrel is the most lovely lake we ever set our eyes upon, filled with trout. His parish is the simple hearted but heroic denizens of this wilderness, and Mr. Beecher is doing

as much good by precept and example as his big brother of world wide fame. Civilization is fast reverting to barbarism and only an adaptation of the same to nature can save it. He is the husband of as noble and self denying a woman as he is a man. Perched away in the top of this Lebanon he is planting a handful of corn that shall shape us another Lebanon. The principles of the man are broader, deeper and more abiding than those of any other Beecher, except, perhaps, his father, the famous trout man of Litchfield. God bless the man true to nature, who loves to go back to his mother earth to fight his way back into the Eden of a restored, because Nature loving, race. A world full of such men and such women as James Beecher and his wife will be Paradise regained.[96]

*James Beecher.*

# 19

## Paradise Lost

James Beecher's sojourn in "Paradise" came to an abrupt end the following fall, in 1881. He was lured away from the Catskills to work for the needy in the slums of Brooklyn by his brother Henry Ward, who in October announced to his congregation at Plymouth Church in Brooklyn that his brother, the Reverend James Beecher, would be in charge of the Plymouth Bethel on Hicks Street, and that he would remain there permanently. James reluctantly agreed to do this, but it turned out to be a bad decision, and he soon suffered what may have been a nervous breakdown.

Plymouth Church operated the mission, which consisted of a multipurpose meeting hall with a dedicated free reading room on the first floor, aimed at educating the working class. Here, working men could read newspapers, magazines, and periodicals of political and religious persuasion, and religious classes and Bible study sessions were held for men and women. The Bethel's main focus, however, was the religious and social education of the many children of the city, to whom they also provided food and clothing. The area of the Bethel was a sprawling community, densely populated, with small streets, tenements, and row houses next to factories, warehouses, docks, and workrooms. For James Beecher, it must have been an enormous change and culture shock, and he did not fare well.

*Plymouth Church interior.*

An assistant of Henry Ward Beecher, the Reverend Samuel B. Halliday, believed the new position overwhelmed James, who came from his quiet retreat in the Catskills and was thrust into the "dizzy whirl" of the work schedule of the Bethel, where daily he viewed the "utmost poverty and suffering." Reverend Halliday believed this situation weighed heavily on James and that because James was prone to melancholia, his health failed. He noticed that James began brooding over his situation and that James claimed he was a burden on society and to his friends.

Rumors of melancholia, a manic-depressive condition inherited from their mother's side of the family, had followed James and his brother Thomas all their lives. Also, it was not uncommon to read about "Beecher eccentricity," and that comment was applied at times to all Beechers. Not too long before he left the Catskills, James Beecher wrote to his wife: "I am sure that there runs a streak of insanity in our Mother's three children, or rather a monomania, assuming diverse forms. I recognize it in Tom and myself. The only advantage I have is in being thoroughly conscious of the fact. Tom is partially so. Belle is absolutely unconscious & is therefore the craziest of the three."[97]

Henry Ward Beecher believed that James was simply overworked, and because he had lived in the country for so long, he could not adjust to the rigors of city life. He was quoted as saying that James had led a quiet life, that he had preached and was a sort of missionary to the people along the upper Beaverkill, and that while he could have continued with that lifestyle, his wife Frances thought he was not using his talents and persuaded him to take charge of the Bethel in Brooklyn. Henry Ward also believed that James was "intensely sympathetic; everybody's care was his care; he wanted to carry everybody's burden, and he could not, and by the end of the year he was all broken up."[98]

James Beecher set high standards for himself as a preacher, and being intensely conscientious, he often could not live up to his own expectations. This in turn caused self-doubt. Yet he was a successful preacher, and the fact that he sometimes filled in at the pulpit of the great Henry Ward Beecher at Plymouth Church proved it. James's sister Harriet Beecher Stowe claimed James was as devout as any Beecher and that he was selfless and spent most of his life helping the underprivileged and those in need.

In 1882, while James was being treated for a liver ailment, a doctor told him that he had serious nerve problems, and he wanted him to consult with a physician in charge of the Middletown State Homeopathic Hospital in Middletown, New York. James met with the physician, who told him that it would be best for him to live at the hospital permanently, because he was subject to a reoccurrence. Instead, James Beecher opted for a trip to Elmira's Water Cure in June, and Frances stayed with him. They lived in Elmira for a month or so and then returned to Beecher Lake. From there, Frances returned to Brooklyn and to the Bethel, where she took up many of the duties previously carried out by her husband.

*Plymouth Bethel on Hicks Street.*

James was living alone at the lake in the fall of 1882 and was visited by his brother Thomas, who brought along a friend who was a physician. Undoubtedly, Thomas did not want James to go through the winter alone, and he and the doctor convinced him to return to the hospital in Middletown in November as a volunteer patient for rest and treatment. It was believed he needed to be under the care of physicians who were specialists in mental disorders. Henry Ward Beecher believed that with rest and quiet, James's health would improve, but he doubted James would ever become strong enough for city life and work.

Being confined to institutions and receiving treatment for a condition that, at the time, was relatively unknown must have been extremely difficult for a man who had been a leader of men, both spiritually and physically. He had spent most of his life helping others, from the crowded slums and back alleys of Canton to Civil War battlefields, where he led men in fierce combat in their fight for freedom, to the backwoods of the upper Beaverkill. Throughout his life, he had experienced tragedy, violence, and poverty, and ultimately, he had found peace and happiness. But now everything was slipping away.

He wrote letters to his wife, Frances, telling her of his love, and he begged her to help him come home before it was too late. Following a visit from her, James wrote Frances to tell her that he should have left with her and could not understand why he did not. He blamed his illness and said at times he was taken over by a "spirit" that was not his own. He also wrote that his illness was like a "strange paralysis" that came over him and that he could be fine one minute, then a feeling pervades his psyche—and then what should he do? He added that being confined in an institution is worse than death and that he trusts no one. He wrote that he would like to write his brother Tom, but he cannot, and asked Frances to tell him that except for his wife he loves Tom better than anything in Heaven or on earth and that he misses him greatly.

In the spring of 1883, James Beecher's health was said to have improved, and news reports claimed he had yielded to the advice of friends and had decided to sell Beecher Lake. However, for the next three years, he was in and out of institutions, primarily between Middletown and Elmira. James spent four agonizing years moving from one institution to another, and he lost his self-esteem. Doctors searched for a cure for his mood swings from euphoria to depression and anxiety, from clear thinking to paranoia. In some ways, he viewed his illness as a slow death, and he felt helpless.

In a letter from Frances to James dated January 31, 1886, she writes, "But do not think for a moment of any one trying, even, to separate us, for they cannot do it, and must know there is no use in trying. I am sure we love each other all the better in many ways for the sorrow we share, as well as the years of joy we have had. Never doubt my heart and my love which is yours only forever."[99]

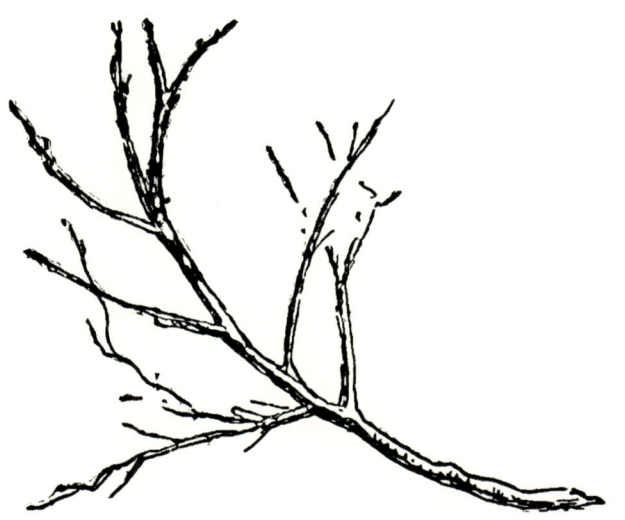

# 20

## The Last Days of James Chaplin Beecher

On August 26, 1886, the *Brooklyn Daily Eagle* reported on the death of the Reverend James Beecher. The newspaper claimed that James had gone to the Elmira Water Cure only recently and was there for "hydropathic treatment" for mental issues that had affected him for some time. He had appeared in fair health, and during the day, he and other patients had enjoyed themselves target shooting at Dr. Gleason's shooting range. Afterward, they got together on the veranda, and at some point, James returned to his room, where he kept his rifle, and took his own life. The newspaper questioned why the managers of the institute allowed patients, especially "Mr. Beecher," whose condition had concerned his friends, to have a rifle in his room.

The article also stated that James was the youngest member of Lyman Beecher's family, all of whom were known for their intellect, accomplishments, and eccentricities, and that he was a sincere and earnest man with great and varied experience:

> He will be remembered with respect and regret by Brooklyn people as the minister of the Plymouth Bethel, in this city. Before that time he had served in China as the pastor of a like institution for sailors. He went to the front, during the Civil War, as chaplain of a regiment, but, as was not surprising in the case of one bearing his name, got himself transferred from the church militant to the more soldierly branch of the service. He comported himself with such courage and energy that he became a colonel, and was mustered out as a brevet brigadier general. He had also tested the hermit's life, and his residence in a lonely region—where he was not a selfish recluse, but one ready to lend a helping hand in any expedient way to those who needed it—is among his recorded eccentricities.[100]

Eccentric, yes—he certainly deviated from the conventional lifestyle of the day. James Beecher was more of a free spirit, a nonconformist, and he spent the vast majority of his life looking out for others and helping the needy and less fortunate. He tried to make their lives better with self-sacrificing deeds. He and Frances helped those in need, not with words, but with acts of kindness, and this kept them as penniless as those they served.

The *New York Times* described the "extremely unique career" of James Beecher claiming "Once he was a power in his church, an ornament of the pulpit, noted less than, but much akin in eloquence to, his half-brother, Henry Ward Beecher."[101]

A column in the *Poughkeepsie Evening Enterprise* on James

Beecher's death reported that the suicide of Reverend Beecher was received with "profound sorrow by his friends and neighbors in the vicinity of his picturesque home in the town of Hardenbergh, Ulster Co.," adding:

> He had endeared himself to the dwellers of that mountainous region by his simple mode of life and his continuous acts of kindness and benevolence. During his entire residence among them he was always ready to help the poor and suffering with hands and money; foremost in every good work, and with all his eccentricity, he was looked upon by those people as a good man, worthy of their highest respect.[102]

Many newspapers eulogized James Beecher. The *Ellenville Journal* reported:

> He did a great amount of good, even in that back settlement. The people grew to love him, and sadly missed him when he left. He preached in the wilderness, for miles and miles away from his home, and the people flocked to hear him, going ten or fifteen miles over the rough roads of that country. He was very kind to the poor, and gave liberally of his means, so that he was always poor of purse.[103]

The newspaper also praised that James Beecher sympathized with his parishioners and was seen as a caring, considerate man, but said that at the Brooklyn Bethel, his wife performed most of the pastoral work and without her assistance, his stay at the mission would have been shorter than it was.

We will never know what haunted James Beecher to take his own life. He experienced many disappointments, tragedies, and the horrors of war, and yet he was frequently filled with compassion for those less fortunate. Being a religious leader, James Beecher was less likely to seek help and to share the pain and grief of war that he carried.

*James Beecher.*

He was said to be as devout as any Beecher and that he was selfless, devoting his late years to helping the poor and needy. At the time of his death, it was written that James was suffering from melancholia that had developed "as the result of sufferings and hardships in the service of his country. It was while suffering from this depressing mental disease that he took his own life."[104]

Years after James's death, his wife, Frances, applied for a pension claiming her husband was afflicted with melancholia. She claimed he contracted the disease while serving in the U.S. Army, that it was caused by the hardships and sufferings he experienced during the Civil War, and that while suffering from this depressing mental illness, he took his own life. Frances Beecher's claim was supported by sworn affidavits that General Beecher contracted the disease while in the service.

An inspector was sent to investigate the case and discovered a memorial pamphlet issued by Frances Beecher that claimed General Beecher had inherited melancholy from his father, Lyman Beecher. The Pension Department then rejected the claim. However, Frances's attorney reminded the Pension Office that the pamphlet brought in by the inspector was unsworn and it was only alleged to have been written by Mrs. Beecher. Frances was later granted a pension of ten dollars a month.

In contemplating James Beecher's taking of his own life, it is conceivable to hypothesize about post-traumatic stress disorder. Civil War veterans were said to carry PTSD for years before being admitted to asylums—their symptoms were similar to those of soldiers today. Unfortunately, PTSD did not enter the medical lexicon until 1980, though its symptoms, including flashbacks, panic attacks, insomnia, and suicidal thoughts turned up frequently among Civil War soldiers, particularly those who entered asylums.

As recently as January of 2015, *Smithsonian Magazine* published an article titled "Did Civil Wars Soldiers Have PTSD?" by journalist Tony Horwitz.[105] The article discusses how historians, clinicians, and genealogists are searching through diaries, letters, hospital files, and even graves at asylum cemeteries for evidence of post-traumatic stress disorder. It seems evident that James C. Beecher was a victim of this awful disease.

Frances Johnson Beecher was an extraordinary woman who shared an intimacy with James Beecher that was far from ordinary. She traveled to a war zone to marry him, then lived for two years as close to the front as she dared, even at times participating in her husband's everyday duties as a colonel of a regiment. She shared in his victories and defeats, his everyday anxieties, and participated in teaching his men to read and write. She, too, was selfless and always put the needs of others before her own.

Before the death of her husband, Frances Beecher opened a private school in Cos Cob, Connecticut, known as the Beecher Family School for Young Girls. Upon the death of James, Frances received a letter of condolence from Frederick Perkins, a widower who lived in San Francisco. Thirty-five years earlier, Frances and Frederick Perkins were betrothed, and their promise to wed was broken by a quarrel. A few years later, Frances married James Beecher, and Frederick Perkins married and moved to San Francisco.

After receiving the letter from Frederick Perkins, Frances and he began corresponding. On a trip to Washington, Perkins visited Frances, and the couple decided to get married in June of 1894, eight years after the death of James Beecher. Unfortunately, the marriage lasted just a few years and ended in the death of Frederick Perkins in 1899.

Even though she had married Perkins, Frances must have

spent a good deal of time reminiscing about her life with James Beecher and the years they spent together. In doing so, she produced two lengthy articles for a literary magazine published in Boston, *The New England Magazine*. The first article was "Two Years with a Colored Regiment" and appeared in 1898. In the second, "A Seven Years Outing," which appeared in 1900, she wrote of the wonderful years she spent living at Beecher Lake. Frances Beecher Perkins died at the age of seventy-one in November 1903 in Brooklyn. She was interred beside her husband, James Chaplin Beecher, at Woodlawn Cemetery in Elmira, New York.

*James and Frances Beecher.*

# Endnotes

### CHAPTER 1

1 Johnson, *John Burroughs Talks*, 37-38.

2 Burroughs, *My Boyhood*, 117-118.

3 Barrus, *The Life and Letters of John Burroughs*, 54.

4 Burroughs, "Birch Browsings," *Atlantic Monthly*, July 1869, 15.

5 Burroughs, "Birch Browsings," *Atlantic Monthly*, July 1869, 21.

6 Ibid, 23.

7 Barrus, *The Life and Letters of John Burroughs*, 140.

8 Burroughs, "The Heart of the Southern Catskills," *The Century*, August 1888, 612.

### CHAPTER 2

9 Knox, *Life and Work of Henry Ward Beecher*, iii.

10 Stowe, *Saints Sinners and Beechers*, 40.

11 Ibid, 384.

12 Bonney, *A Legacy of Historical Gleanings*, 233.

### CHAPTER 3

13 Rugoff, *The Beechers: An American Family in the Nineteenth Century*, 452.

14 Ibid, 451.

15 *The Sailor's Magazine*, June 1858, 20.

16 Rugoff, *The Beechers: An American Family in the Nineteenth Century*, 452.

17 Letter from Rev. J. C. Beecher, *The Sailor's Magazine*, February 1858, 162.

18 *American Seaman's Friend Society Thirty-Second Annual Report*, 1860, 22-25.

19    Rugoff, *The Beechers: An American Family in the Nineteenth Century*, 454.

## Chapter 4

20    Civil War Trust, "Answers to your Civil War Questions," www.civilwar.org/education/history/faq.

21    Letter from James C. Beecher to Harriet Beecher Stowe, January 27, 1862.

22    *Soldiers and Patriots Biographical Album*, 291-292.

23    The Union Army: A History of Military Affairs in the Loyal States, 1861-1865 vol. 6, Cyclopedia of Battles, 935-938.

24    Letter from James C. Beecher to Isabella Beecher, June 7, 1862.

25    Ibid.

26    Ibid.

27    Horwitz, "Did Civil War Soldiers Have PTSD?," *Smithsonian Magazine*, January 2015.

## Chapter 5

28    Civil War Trust, "July 1, 1862: The Battle of Malvern Hill," www.battlefields.org/learn/articles/malvern-hill.

29    *Christian Union*, December 31, 1879, 577.

## Chapter 7

30    Hutchins, *A History of the 35th United States Colored Troops 1863-1866*.

31    Richard, *North Carolina Historical Review*, "Raising the African Brigade: Early Black Recruitment in Civil War North Carolina," July 1993, 277-284.

32    *Hartford Evening Press*, March 5, 1864; New England Loyal Publication Society, March 19, 1864.

33    *The Liberator*, "Gen. Wild's Brigade," July 17, 1863, 115.

34     *Hartford Evening Press*, March 5, 1864; New England
      Loyal Publication Society, March 19, 1864.

35     Letter from James C. Beecher to Frances Johnson, June 26, 1863.

36     Hedrick, *Harriet Beecher Stowe: A Life*, 305.

37     *New York Times*, "The First Regiment North Carolina
      Colored Volunteers – Flag Presentation," 1.

CHAPTER 8

38     Emilio, *A Brave Black Regiment: History of the Fifty-Fourth Regiment of*
      *Massachusetts Volunteer Infantry, 1863-1865*, 81.

39     Ibid, 83.

40     Pohanka, "Fort Wagner and the 54th Massachusetts
      Volunteer Infantry," America's Civil War Magazine.

41     Emilio, A Brave Black Regiment: History of the Fifty-Fourth Regiment
      of Massachusetts Volunteer Infantry 1863-1865, 77.

42     Williams, *A History of the Negro Troops in the*
      *War of the Rebellion 1861-1865*, 195.

43     Lange, "Meet Sgt. William Carney: The First African-American Medal
      of Honor recipient," Department of Defense News, Defense Media
      Activity, February 10, 2017.

44     Washington, *The Story of the Negro*, 330.

45     Helmuth, *A System of Surgery*, 215-216.

46     Ibid.

47     *Harper's Weekly*, "Treatment of Captured Colored Soldiers,"
      August 15, 1863, 514-515.

48     Williams, *A History of the Negro Troops in the*
      *War of the Rebellion 1861-1865*, 202-203.

CHAPTER 9

49     Letter from James C. Beecher to Frances Johnson, August 28, 1863.

50   Letter from Colonel Beecher to Brig, Gen. Wild, September 13, 1863.

51   Letter from James C. Beecher to Senator Henry Wilson,
     January 13, 1864.

52   Ibid.

53   *Hartford Evening Press*, March 5, 1864.

CHAPTER 10

54   Allman, *The True History of the Sunshine State*, 232.

55   Letter from James C. Beecher to Frances Johnson, March 16, 1864.

56   Letter from James C. Beecher to Frances Johnson, March 26, 1864.

57   Letter from James C. Beecher to Frances Johnson, April 4, 1864.

58   Letter from James C. Beecher to Frances Johnson, April 15, 1864.

59   Letter from James C. Beecher to Frances Johnson, June 1, 1864.

60   Hutchins, *A History of the 35th United States
     Colored Troops 1863-1866.*

61   Perkins, "Two Years with a Colored Regiment:
     A Woman's Experience," *New England Magazine*, 535.

CHAPTER 11

62   *New York Times*, "The War in Georgia," December 9, 1864, 1.

63   Letter from James C. Beecher to Frances Beecher, December 2, 1864.

64   Williams, *A History of the Negro Troops in the
     War of the Rebellion, 1861-1863*, 211-213.

65   Letter from Z. Platt to Rev. Henry Ward Beecher, December 16, 1864.

CHAPTER 12

66   Letter from James C. Beecher to Frances Beecher, February 19, 1865.

67   *New York Times*, "Slavery's Enduring Resonance," March 14, 2105, SR 5.

68   Olajide, *The Complete Concise History of the Slave Trade*, 44-45.

69   Perkins, "Two Years with a Colored Regiment:
     A Woman's Experience," *New England Magazine*, 539.

## Chapter 13

70    Ibid, 542.

71    Ibid, 543.

72    Letter from James C. Beecher to O. D. Kinsman, October 29, 1865.

73    *Semi Weekly Louisianan*, December 10, 1871, 1.

## Chapter 14

74    *New York Times*, "Some Hit and Miss Chat," August 27, 1886.

75    Rugoff, *The Beechers: An American Family in the
      Nineteenth Century*, 462.

76    Ibid, 445.

77    Tillson, Map of Ulster County, New York, 1858,
      https://www.loc.gov/item/2013593238/.

78    Beers, County atlas of Sullivan, New York, 1875,
      https://www.loc.gov/item/2013593063/.

79    *Christian Union*, "In the Woods," September 9, 1874, 183.

80    Ibid.

## Chapter 15

81    Perkins, "A Seven Years Outing," *New England Magazine*,
      July 1900, 593.

82    *Catskill Examiner*, September 8, 1877, 1.

83    Ibid.

## Chapter 16

84    *Hartford Weekly Times*, "Trout Fishing in the Woods,"
      August 2, 1877, 6.

85    Ibid.

86    Ibid.

87    Perkins, "A Seven Years Outing," *New England Magazine*,
      July 1900, 593.

88    *Kingston Weekly Freeman*, September 2, 1886, p. 3.

89    Perkins, "A Seven Years Outing," *New England Magazine*,
      July 1900, 595.

90    Ibid.

CHAPTER 17

91    Ibid, 601.

92    Plumley, *With the Trout Fly*, 29.

93    *Bismarck Weekly Tribune* (North Dakota), April 12, 1878, 1.

CHAPTER 18

94    Reprinted in the *Catskill Examiner*, September 8, 1877, 1.

95    Judd, "Beecher's Clearing," *American Agriculturist*,
      September 1881, 354-356.

96    *Brooklyn Daily Eagle*, "The Willowemoc Region,"
      August 26, 1880, 1.

CHAPTER 19

97    Letter from James C. Beecher to Frances Beecher, March 20, 1880.

98    *Perry Herald*, "Rev. James Beecher," December 14, 1882, 1.

99    Rugoff, *The Beechers: An American Family in the
      Nineteenth Century*, 465.

CHAPTER 20

100   *Brooklyn Daily Eagle*, "The Suicide of Rev. James C. Beecher,"
      August 26, 1886, 2.

101   *New York Times*, "James C. Beecher's Suicide," August 26, 1886, 1.

102   *Poughkeepsie Evening Enterprise*, "James C. Beecher's Suicide," August
      27, 1886, 2.

103   *Ellenville Journal,* "The Hermit Preacher," September 13, 1886.

104   *Sunday Morning Globe,* "Up To Teddy?" October 20, 1901, 5.

105   Horwitz, "Did Civil War Soldiers Have PTSD?",
      *Smithsonian Magazine,* January 2015.

*Selected correspondence of James Beecher*

Camp 1st Reg.t Long Island Vols
Washington 27th Jan.y 1862

Dear Hattie

Your welcome note is just at hand
and as I am tired out with a week of extra hard
work – and thereby in a fit of the blues – which
forbid sleeping, It seems as though the nearest
I can come to a pleasant talk with you, is to
answer your letter at once. Your letter is very
welcome, dear Hattie – and yet every new recog-
nition which comes in shape of kind words,
makes me so long for a visit to old friends, that
I feel sad at being kept away. I came
home from China, where I was in some respects very
pleasantly situated – Found a place in the army
at once & went into it. Nobody wrote to me – or
seemed to care for me, so I said – Well the
folks have all forgotten me and my only real
friends are in China. Under these circumstances I was just fit for a soldier – and had we
been permitted to come into action – I believe
that a chaplain would have been found about
as near the front – as any officer in the Service. But now from one & another – come
letters – long delayed – which bring back vividly
my life before going to China, and the love
of past time – grows anew. I cannot realize

that it is six years since I was in Andover

In the press of constant duty, and in a foreign friend I had forgotten many a scene of Andover life which your note recalls. To-night in my tent. I can recall a thousand memories which had gone long ago — I can see the old Stone House & garden — nay. I can see you writing the note before me — Though a photograph which I saw at Brooklyn told me that you were somewhat altered.

It is strange how a line from a friend awakens remembrances.

I have made up my mind for a pleasant visit to Andover. It would do me good I know for the older I grow — (and alas! I am thirty four now) The more I cling to the affection of those around me. But. I promised the Plymouth Church at Chicago, that I would come on & spend some days with them — on their invitation — and now I must go — instead of going eastward — as I had hoped & intended — in case the Chicago plan was not carried out. However I mean to accomplish it yet. if possible.

There is a camp rumor to-day that we are to go on a new expedition somewhere down South. Of course if any active service turns up. I shall stay by my Regt. But if nothing active goes on. I intend to visit Hartford and Andover — After fulfilling my engagement at

Chicago – before rejoining my Regt.

I am very glad that my ideas of Fred's promotion – are acceptable – for I half feared lest that which was well meant on my part might seem an intrusion. — I was taken quite aback, when Col Green broached the subject of Fred's Lieutenancy, and could only say that which I would have said in behalf of my own son.

By the way – I am urged to resign my chaplaincy – & accept command of a Rifle Company – consisting of picked men from the Regiment. Had John Bull proceeded to fight – after our very proper action in the Bent affair – I would not have hesitated a moment for I believe that in two months time I could drill a company with the rifle. So that a volley would be a damage to an enemy.

As it is, should I not conclude to go to Chicago. I shall probably take a company & do what one man may towards damaging our "Southern brethren."

I had heard of Susan Arch's marriage – and knew Sturgis for some years in China. I should prefer that a sister or child of mine should marry almost any body else. Yet after all perhaps it matters little. If there is no capacity for love on either side & plenty of money

for support. (which I take to be the case
in the present instance) perhaps the
parties are far better off than with love
poverty and a dozen other trials.

   I still hope to have a weeks
pleasure with you and other loved ones
in Andover. I must go to Chicago on
the 5ᵗʰ of Feby. & remain ten days. I
shall take twenty one days furlough, and
in case our Regt is not called into action. I hope to go on to Hartford from Chicago
Thence to Andover.   I remember our
friendship at Andover, dear Hatter
with great pleasure and am glad you
have not entirely forgotten it. I know
you are not fond of letter writing, yet you
must try to overcome your dislike. and
write to me for you have no idea how welcome
letters are in Camp life. Love to Elsie
and Georgie. And believe me
  — Ever Affectionately Yours
    J. C. Beecher.

Before the evening 1/2 mile
north east of Fair Oak Station
on Richmond R.R. June 7th

Dear Isabel

When the fight was at
Williamsburg & our boys for 10 hours
had held against all odds. Gen. Mc
Clellan could only learn that Gen. Hancock had made a charge of bayonets.

In the fight of 31st May – he being
up in two balloons only found out
that Gen. Casey's division broke dis-
 unitedly – and that Gen. Heintzleman
came up & saved the day. He does
not yet know that Gen. Couch's division
in rear of Gen. Casey. held for four
hours. The flower of the enemy in
check – Though out flanked. out
generaled & out maneuvered every way

Unfortunately I was not up in
two balloons. and hence my
views are less comprehensive.

The fight commenced on ~~Saturday~~

Before the enemy ½ mile northeast of Fair Oak Station

on Richmond R.R. June 7 (1862)

Dear Isabella,

When the fight was at Williamsburg & our boys for 10

hours had held against all odds, Gen. McClellan could only learn

that Gen. Hancock had made a charge of bayonets.

In the fight of 31st May - he being up in two balloons only

found out that Gen. Casey's division broke initially - and that Gen.

Heintzelman came up and saved the day. He does not yet know that

Gen. Couch's division in rear of Gen. Casey, held for four hours, the

flood of the enemy in check - though out flanked, out generaled, &

out maneuvered every way.

Unfortunately I was not up in two balloons, and hence my

views are less comprehensive.

The fight commenced on Saturday  (*cont.*)

2

by the complete surprise of Gen
Casey's division which was the
advance of our extreme left. Gen
McC to the contrary in his despatch
saying it was on the right flank of
the Army. — The right flank was
Six miles distant & was not engaged
at all. — Our division was in
rear of Casey. ½ mile & when
the firing commenced it formed in
line of battle — and had hardly
done so, when like sheep the advance
division came through us with
exaggerated tales of their defeat
And here I take up my own Regt
as I had better time to see what
else happened. — I was acting as
Col's Aide — & by his order — halted
the fugitives in rear of our line
untill the enemy were upon us
then I went in with my own
men. — For 1½ hours we were
exposed to a fearful fire of

by the complete surprise of Gen. Casey's division which was the

advance of our extreme left. Gen. Mc. to the contrary in his dispatch

saying it was on the right flank of the army. The right flank was six

miles distant & was not engaged well. Our division was in rear of

Casey, ½ mile & when the firing commenced or formed in line of

battle and had hardly done so when like sheep the advance division

came through us with exaggerated tales of their defeat and here I

take up my own Regt. as I had little time to see what else happened.

I was riding as Cols. Aide & by his orders rallied other fugitives in

rear of our line until the enemy was upon us.

Then I went in with my own men. For 1 ½ hours we were

exposed to a fearful fire of    (*cont.*)

artillery — to which our battery responded
& from which we lost several.

Then the Regt on our right having
been driven back, Colo Adams requested
me to ride down to the right & see
if we were not being out flanked.

I rode down on the jump &
rode right into the enemy, coming
up by the road & through the swamp
At least a hundred shots were
fired at me but, riding back
we wheeled our right wing so
as to enfilade the road. The
bushes were so thick that we couldn't
see the enemy until within sixty
or seventy yds. & then we opened on
them. There were five Regts en
gaged — and we only mustered 500
men, one company being absent.

We fought well. How I came
out I know not. My boys are
falling like leaves. Then

artillery, to which our battery responded & from which we lost several.

Then the Regt. on our right having been turned back, Col. Adams requested me to ride down to the right & see if we were not being out flanked.

I rode down on the jump & rode right into the enemy, coming up by the road & through the swamp.

At least a hundred shots were fired at me but riding back we wheeled on right doing so as to emplace the road. The bushes were so thick that we couldn't see the enemy until within sixty or seventy yds. & then we opened on them. There were four Regts. engaged, and we only mustered 500 men, one company being absent.

We fought well. How I came out I know not. My boys were falling like leaves. Then      *(cont.)*

4

it became evident that the enemy
had got past our flank & were
coming round to surround us.

The order was given to fall
back. We did so. Then
Rallied again & the Colors
& fought till our battery was
safely retired, & then sulkily
& unwillingly filed out & retired
to the rifle pits a short distance
in the rear. "The enemy did
not follow". And Heintzelman's
relief did not come until we
had done the work — in that
spot. As soon as we had
retired I went to work with
wounded — was up all Saturday
night — Sunday & Sunday night
On Monday morning went back
to battlefield ground & brought our
dead. Nobody fought but
Heintzelman forsooth!

it became evident that the enemy had got past our flank & were coming round to surround us.

The order was given to fall back, we did so. Then called again to the colors & fought till our battery was safely retired & then sulkily & unwillingly fled out & retired to the rifle pits a short distance in the rear. "The enemy did not follow." And Heintzelman's relief did not come until we had done the work, in that spot.

As soon as we had retired I went to work with wounded, was up all Saturday night, Sunday & Sunday night.

On Monday morning went back to battle ground & found our dead. Nobody but Heintzelman's forsooth!    *(cont.)*

Why thirty three of my brave boys —
lie there under that ground and
One hundred & thirty six wounded
have gone to Hospital. and this
out. of 500 engaged — "we don't
count up on "missing". All who
are not killed & wounded are in
the ranks again. Here we are
in the advance once more hoping
that the ASS who leads the Union
forces may sometime find out that
there is some one, in service harder Gen Hancock
& Gen Heintzleman. In front
of our fighting ground. I counted in
space of sixty yds over thirty rebel
dead and an Officer of the 2nd New
Hampshire Regt. now camped
there tells me that they had
a days work burying the Rebels
before they could make their
Camp. No — Sister Bella
when the real history of this war
is written — if ever it is.

Why thirty-three of my brave boys lie there under that ground and one hundred & thirty-six wounded have gone to hospital, and this out of 500 engaged we don't count up on "missing."

All who are not killed & wounded are in the ranks again. There we are in the advance once more hoping that the ASS who leads the Union forces may sometimes force out that there is some-one in service beside Gen. Hancock & Gen. Heintzelman.

In front of our fighting ground, I counted in space of sixty yds. Over thirty rebels dead and an officer of the 2nd New Hamp-shire Regt., now camped there tells me that they had a days work burying the rebels before they could make their camp. No, sister Bella when the real history of this war is written, if ever it is,

(*cont.*)

it will not be from McClellan despatches
or N.Y. Herald lying Correspondents
which are the same thing —  And
I only write this — That in Case I am
killed in the next fight — I may
have testified to the bravery of
my boys — and the desperate fight
they made, Gen Couches disp.
at thus will I suppose place his
division in its proper light and
in Course of a week or so Gen
Mc will come down from his two
balloons — & learn for the first time
that brave men fought & died
fighting to hold the ground
which his stupidly left only
half guarded.

It day the sun comes out for
first time since Monday last
I have slept on the ground
til my back aches — and arms
grow ~~stiff~~ — Yet if only we may

it will not be from McClellan descriptions or N. Y. Herald lying correspondents which are the same thing. And I only wish this, that in case I'm killed in the next fight, I may have testified to the bravery of my boys, and the desperate fight they made. Gen. Couch's dispatcher will I suppose place his division in its proper light and in course of a week or so Gen. Mc. will come from his two balloons & have for the first time that brave men fought & died fighting to hold the ground which his stupidity left only half guarded.

Today the sun comes out for the first time since Monday last.

I have slept on the ground till my back aches, and arms grow stiff. Yet if only we may      (*cont.*)

next time have half a chance at
the enemy — be informed of
his approach & the direction of it
and more than all catch him
out of these infernal Swamps — I
feel sure we will give good account
of him — & then — "Hail McClellan"
Bah !!

We are camped on a battle
field — then Sumner came up
on Sunday — Every tree is shattered
more or less — & huge trenches filled
with Rebel dead are on every side

From a space ½ mile square —
1173 dead Rebels have been gathered,
a fearful harvest. And yet
I grieve more over my thirty three
slain than glory over the thousands
of the enemy — I saw them fall
Many of them I knew just where
to look for when the battle was
done — Poor fellows ! Yet I
think more sorrowfully of those

next time have half a chance at the enemy, be informed of his approach & the direction of it and more than all catch him out of these infernal swamps. I feel sure we will give account of him & then "<u>Hail</u> <u>McClellan</u>" Bah!!

We are camped on a battlefield, where (Gen.) Sumner comes up on Sunday. Enemy here is shattered more or less, & huge trenches filled with Rebel dead and on every side.

From a space ½ mile square 1,173 dead rebels have been gathered, a fearful harvest. And yet I grieve some over my thirty-three slain than glory over the thousands of the enemy. I saw them fall, many of them I knew just where to look for when the battle was done. Poor fellows! & yet I think more sorrowfully of those

(*cont.*)

8

they have left behind. — Yesterday
I was distributing the mail &c.
all came back upon me. for
letter after letter was for some one
whose eyes would never read more

Ah well. — So the world
goes. — Orders come to
fall into line. The enemy
are not far off —. It may
be that in an hour time
we go through the furnace
again. I only wish the
~Northern~
~mercenary~ politicians were
in our front rank — or in
the front rank of the enemy
I care little which —

Love to the girls — Send
this to Sister Catie who is
at Guilford I believe & to
Cousin Frankie Johnson, who is
there too. I cant write much
more often just now.
Lovingly am Jas. J. C. B.

they have left behind. Yesterday I was distributing the mail & it and it all came back upon me, for letter after letter was for someone whose eyes would never read more.

Ah well, so the world goes. Orders came to fall into line. The enemy are not far off. It may be that in an hours time we go through the furnace again. I only wish the Northern slavery politicians were in our front rank, or in the first rank of the enemy I care little which.

Love to the girls – send this to sister Cate who is at Milford I believe & to Cousin Frankie Johnson who is there too. I can't write much more often just now.

Lovingly Ever Yrs.

J. C. B.

*In margin*: In all New York papers the 1st Long Island Regiment will appear as the 67th New York.

Hea'd qrs 1st N.C.C. Vols

Folly Island Aug. 28th 1863

My dear Frances

It is the first mail I have had ...

that being ordered hither upon the letter channel
is broken up & one has to wait so for letters. Not
a word have I had for near three weeks. Scarcely
a newspaper even. Then nothing seems to
go direct. If letters go at all they lie round
until some chance Steamer goes to Helen Head
& then are trundled around there until some
boat is sent to Fortress Monroe or somewhere
else for stores. I am starving for letters. I'd give
all the glory of the campaign for a regular mail
as well. The last week has been a succession of
heavy rains interspersed with clear cool weather
far cooler than at the north. A good blanket at
night is not out of place. The seige goes so so. as
I wrote you before. The monitors are double refined
humbugs. Everybody is scouting them. Today I have
been to the front. along with the Sharp Shooters. close
on to "Wagner". & 3000 yds from Sumpter. Our batteries

August 28, 1863 Folly Island

My dear Frankie,

It is this great trial of solders life that being ordered hither & yon the letter channel is broken up & one has to wait on few letters. Not a word have I had for near three weeks. Scarcely a newspaper even. Then nothing seems to go direct. If letters go at all they lie around until some chance steamer goes to Hilton Head then are trundled around there until some boat is sent to Fortress Monroe or somewhere else for stores. I am starving for letters. I'd give all the glory of the campaign for a regular mail well. The last week has been a succession of heavy rains interspersed with clear cool weather far cooler than at the north. A good blanket at night is not out of place. The siege goes so-so – as I wrote you before. The munitions are double refined humbugs. Everybody is scouting them. Today I have been to the front along with the sharpshooters close on to "Wagners" & 300+ guns from Sumpter. Our batteries

(*cont.*)

rendered the latter harmless. There is no practicable
breach. but the whole South & East faces are so
hammered & battered that they are of no service
and the guns are dismounted save 3 or 4. the
fort does not fire. and has not over 50 men in it
Fort Gregg is a contemptible little sand bank
about 60 ft in diameter. with five guns. one of
which was handsomely knocked out of the embrasure
by a shot from the 800 pdr. almost under my nose
so near did my glass make it seem. Fort Wagner
is a tumbled up mess of sand bags & loose sand
mounting 8 or 10 guns. & yet there lie Six Monitors
and huge Ironsides. & dont dare to come near

The sharp shooters of both sides are perched in all
sorts of nondescript holes & firing through cracks in every
direction. It is one continued pop. pop. and a
man cant show half his head without getting a ball
through it. I saw one poor fellow shot right through the
heart. I detest this little sneaking way of fighting.
and as I had no business at the front except to learn
the Situation. I didnt stay longer than was necessary
for a good careful survey. I heard enough of that
villanous ball whistling on the Peninsula.

From all I can see, I see no reason to doubt
the accuracy of what I last wrote. We are no

rendered the latter harmless. There is no practicable breach but the whole south & east faces are so hammered & battered that they are of no service and the guns are dismounted save 3 or 4 – the fort does not fire- and has not over 50 men in it Fort Gregg is a contemptible little sandbank about 60 ft. in diameter – with five guns – one of which was handsomely knocked out of the embrasure by a shot from the 300 pd – almost under my nose so near did any glass make it seem. Fort Wagner is tumbled up mess of sand bags & loose sand mounting 8 or 10 guns - & yet these six monitors and huge Ironside & don't dare to come near.

The sharp shooters of both sides are perched in all sorts of nondescript holes & firing through cracks in every direction. It is one continued pop-pop, and a man can't show half his head without getting a ball through it. I saw one poor fellow shot right through the heart. I detest this little sneaking way of fighting, and as I had no business at the front except I knew the situation. I didn't stay longer than was necessary for a good careful survey. I heard enough of that villainous ball whistling on the Peninsula.

From all I can see, I do not see reason to doubt The accuracy of what I last wrote. We are no     *(cont.)*

nearer to taking Charleston than we were six months
ago. No doubt Gen Gilmore is an excellent Officer
but there is a screw loose somewhere. The enemy
meanwhile are building two batteries to our one.
All the north of James island is becoming a continuous
line of fortification. I watch them growing from day to
day. and shall be surprised if we do not find our
present quarters too hot to hold us. let alone making
any advance. I fear you will think I'm a croaker. but
the event will show. Meanwhile I have worked hard
to get my regiment in comfortable quarters & have succeeded admirably. There is not a better camp in
the department or more cleanly. my sick list has decreased one half among the men. I'm troubled about the
Officers. One has died. two are dangerously sick. four
more are complaining among whom are the Lieut
Col. We have poor food & no cooking utensils. My
Kitchen furniture consists of 1 Coffee Pot. 1 Sauce pan and
two Shovels to fry pork & flap jacks in. I was crazy to
leave my nice little mess chest. but I had to think
of the Regt & had no poor servant to look out for me
In a week or so I shall be out of money & out at elbows
unless our baggage comes from New Berne. Altogether
I don't like it a bit. for there was no necessity for

nearer to taking Charleston than we were six months ago. No doubt Gen. Gilmore is an excellent officer but there is a screw loose somewhere. The enemy meanwhile are building two batteries to our one.

All the north of James Island is becoming a continuous line of fortification. I watch them growing from day to day. And shall be surprised if we do not find our present quarters too hot to hold us – Let alone making any advance. I fear you will think I'm a croaker – but the event will show. Meanwhile I have worked hard to get my regiment in comfortable quarters & have succeded admirably. There is not a better camp in the department or more cleanly. My sick list has decreased one half among the men. I'm troubled about the officers. One has died. Two are dangerously sick – four more are complaining among whom are the Lieut Col. We have poor food & no cooking utensils. My kitchen furniture consists of 1 coffee pot, 1 saucepan and two shovels I fry pork & flapjacks in – I was crazy to leave my nice little mess chest but I had to think of the Regt & had no good servant to look out for me.

In a week or so I shall be out of money & out at elbows unless our baggage comes from New Bern. Altogether I don't like it a bit – for there was no necessity for       (*cont.*)

hustling us off in this stupid way.

29th　Stopped writing & went to sleep soundly My bed consists of four slakes with a board across. a rubber poncho & wool blanket. It's a little rough on the bones - especially when one is losing flesh. at rate of 2 lbs per week. I weighed 147 this am against 158 at New Berne. The Lieut Col says he has lost more in weight and I don't doubt it. the weather is beautiful - clean as a bell and not very hot. Little firing from either side I think we are short of ammunition.

Sunday Evg. Fine batch of letters from New Berne. Yours & Belle's of 29th July - mailed 30th This was the very day on which I hustled off at 3 hours notice. for Charleston - There are three letters from Belle. all about Mr Burton - I'm sorry for the disappointment - but this is the first I have seen about the application - and it is too late to do anything. I am annoyed too about Allen. I had two applications for the Commission either of which would have suited me equally well but friend Warner seemed to feel an interest in Allens appointment and so I nominated him. Just my luck. I am short of officers - and Expect to be still shorter - for somehow this climate don't agree with them very well. I'm glad you like Anna Dickinson. "my dear prophetess". We met under peculiar circumstances. She worn out and sick from the excitement of political campaigning - I broken down & unmanned by the hard ordeal through which I had passed. We both wanted rest - and in that quiet hustling us off in this stupid way.

29th    Stopped writing & went to sleep soundly. My bed consists of four stakes with a board across,

a rubber poncho & wool blanket. It's a little rough on the bones – especially when one is losing flesh at the rate of 2 lbs per week. I weighed 147 this AM against 158 at New Berne. The Lieut Col says he has lost over 30 lbs weight and I don't doubt it.

The weather is beautiful – clear as a bell and not very hot. Little firing from either side I think we are short of the ammunition. Sunday Eve.    Fine batch of letters from New Bern yours & Belles of 29th July. Mailed 30th This was the very day on which I hustled off at 3 hours notice for Charleston. There are three letters from Belle – all about Mr. Benton – I'm sorry for the disappointment – but this is the first I have seen about the application – and it is too late to do anything. I am annoyed too about Allen. I had two applications for the commission either of which would have suited me equally well but friend Warner seemed to feel an interest in Allen's appointment and so I nominated him just my luck. I am short of officers – and expect to be still shorter – for somehow this climate don't agree with them very well. I'm glad you like Anna Dickenson "my dear prophetess." We met under peculiar circumstances. She worn out and sick from the excitement of political campaigning. I

broken down & unmanned by the hard ordeal through which I had passed. We both wanted rest – and in that quiet    *(cont.)*

Brook-Farm. as found it. I believe that on my part
at least. without any of the nonsense which somehow
seems incidental to the association of men &women (except
when engaged) I learned to love her sincerely and
truly and I believe she is worthy of any body's love.
There is something peculiarly winning about her. My old.
Surgeon. Says that "Miss Anna Dickenson" is a flirt &c.
whereupon I metaphorically boxed the old gentleman's
ears. at a venture. I think she is mistaken in
her expressed ideas of love &c. for while professing a
kind of indifference. and lack of conception of any
thing like like love in respect to courtship &all that
I believe that when she found the man of her choice
one worthy of her. She would love with all the power
of a true woman's heart &for him would bear all
things and endure all things. And so dear,
Frankie. to my Affianced wife. I say that I love
Anna the prophetess dearly and am right glad that
you are too. _ _ _ _         10 P.M. Have just been
up in my look out to watch the firing. which at times
is quite brisk. I think there is something up. as
the shelling is at short range. Our own men in the
trenches tonight so can look on without personal anx
iety. "Selfish!" you say. Well so it is positively but not
Comparatively. I feel so peculiarly anxious. when my boys
are under fire. That Comparatively speaking Im quite

Nook-farm – we found it. I believe that on my part at least without any of the nonsense which somehow seems incidental to the association of men & women (except when engaged) I learned to love her sincerely and truly and I believe she is worth of anybody's love – There is something peculiarly winning about her. My old Surgeon says that "Miss Anna Dickenson" is a flirt etc. whereupon I metaphorically boxed the old gentlemans ears – at a venture. I think she is mistaken in her expressed ideas of love etc. for which professing a kind of indifference and lack of conception of any thing like like love in respect to courtship & all that I believe that when she found the man of her choice one worthy of her – she would love with all the power of a true womans heart & for him would bear all things and endure all things – and so dear, Frankie – to my affianced wife – I say that I love Anna the prophetess dearly and am right glad that You do too. - - - 10 P.M. – Have just been up in my lookout to watch the firing - which at times is quite brisk. I think there is something up. As the shelling is at short range. Ive no men in the trenches tonight so I can look on without personal anxiety. "Selfish!" you say. Well so it is positively but not comparatively. I feel so peculiarly anxious. When my boys are under fire. That comparatively speaking I'm quite     *(cont.)*

Careless when other boys are on duty. It's the tendency
of military life to concentrate ones ideas and make
him apparently though not really selfish. I'm the representative of you & odd men. I'm responsible for everything
connected with them. The Gen'l don't know anything
about you men. he knows only 1st Reg't N.C.C.V. Col Beecher. So as it uses about all the ability any one
man has to Camp. discipline. work = fight and
look generally after you. The Colonel naturally
makes that you his little world & knows or cares
little what takes place outside & if every Colonel
does this. then all the soldiers will be looked after
But as I was writing. My Frankie is too much
of a (true) woman to love the prophetess less. because
I love her too. ~~Bye~~ I'm making a long letter. and
have got at least five business. Camp letters to
answer from New Bern. I wish I could diagram
all our positions here so that you could see how we
are working. but that is against orders. All is. You
must be patient. Know that the correspondent of the
Herald. invariably lies. Correspondent of Associated
Press ditto. The truth is simply this. Sumpter is not breached
though it is useless to the enemy. being so hammered that
not more than four guns are or can be mounted
Fort Wagner is a hard nut. to crack. and the

careless when other boys are on duty. It's the tendency of military life to concentrate one's ideas and make men apparently though not really selfish. Im the represen tative of 900+odd men. I'm responsible for everything connected with them. The Gen'l don't know anything about 900 men. He knows only 1st Regt. N.C.C.V. Col Beecher. So as it uses about all the ability any one man has to camp discipline – work – fight – and look generally after 900 – The Colonel naturally makes that 900 his little world & knows or cares little what takes place outside & if every Colonel does this – then all the soldiers will be looked after. But as I was writing – My Frankie is too much of a (true) woman to love the prophetess less – because I love her too. I'm making a long letter – and have got at least five business camp letters to answer from New Berne. I wish I could diagram all our positions here so that you could see how we are working – but that is against orders – all is – you must be patient – know that the correspondent of the Herald – invariably lies – Correspondent of Associated Press ditto. The truth is simply this – Sumpter is not breached. Though it is useless to the enemy – being so hammered that not more than four guns are or can be mounted.

Fort Wagner is a hard nut to crack. and the (*cont.*)

gun boats are useless. utterly so thus far. they are afraid to come within range. We have shelled Charleston from one gun — but it burst. We shall do better in course of 48 hours. if nothing unforseen happens. I believe we can destroy the city. but as I wrote before — It will take until November to dig up to it or throw forces into it and that is about the whole of it.

Sept 1st Was on duty all day yesterday as General Officer of the day. Had to ride a good many miles & visit several brigades — but was paid for my trouble by seeing & hearing generally. Had a neat little fight in P. M. between 3 monitors & the forts. Am more than ever impressed with their utter uselessness against land batteries. They stood the fire of Wagner — Moultrie & "battery B." for an hour or so. then mizzled ingloriously. They fired on an average about one shot to twenty from the enemy. and at intervals of about 15 to 20 minutes. Was scared a little by an attack of dysentery — which is laying up so many men & officers. Thought my turn had come at last. Starved for 36 hours. worked to keep from thinking about it and am all right today.

Midnight. A grand bombardment has been going on since 10 P.M. It was rumored today that gun boats are useless. Utterly so thus far. They are afraid to come within range. We have shelled Charleston from one gun but it burst. We shall do better in course of 218 hours. If nothing unforeseen happens. I believe we can destroy the city. But as I wrote before – it will take until November to dig up to it or throw forces into it and that is about the whole of it.

Sept. 1st Was on duty all day yesterday as General officer of the day. Had to ride a good many miles & visit several brigades – but was paid for my trouble by seeing & hearing generally. Had a neat little fight in P.M. between 3 monitors & the forts – am more than even impressed with their utter uselessness against land batteries – They stood the fire of Wagner, Moultrie & "battery B" for an hour or so. Then muzzled ingloriously – They fired on an average about one shot to twenty from the enemy. And at intervals of about 10 to 20 minutes. Was scared a little by an attach of dystentery – which is laying up so many men & officers – thought my time had come at last – starved for 36 hours – worked to keep from thinking about it an am all right today.

<u>Midnight.</u>     A grand bombardment has been going on since 10 P.M. It was rumoured today that     *(cont.)*

Admiral Farragut had come down. Somebody's come, I
should say for the monitors are really fighting for the first
time since I've been here — How I wish you were here
dear Frankie. It's bright moonlight — clear & cold, so
cold that I got numb on my lookout & had to come
down to warm. The deep round crash of our big guns
is tremendous. Just think — 2 batteries of 200 prs.
one 300 pdr. Six Monitors with 15 inch guns, & old
Ironsides with her huge battery all flashing & roaring
away like mad. The enemies fire was incessant
at first — but has mainly died up — I think somebody
is hurt. Shall hope to see a bigger hole in Sumter
than ever before. I shouldn't wonder if soldiers are
wanted in the morning for some storming.
    Sumter has not fired a gun. it is done up for
this campaign. I've seen a good deal of powder
burned. but I never heard anything so grand as the
roll of these monster guns.
    2 A.M. Sept 2nd. Have been round getting up all my
camp guard in case the enemy should make a dash
at daylight on Folly Island while the gun boats are
busy in Light House inlet. Don't know as I can do
any more. So laying out round & revolver handy — till we
have a nap spite of the guns.
    9 A.M. Was out at sunrise on my lookout to see
what was up. Alas, nothing — as usual. I've scanned
their work. Sumter is as the land batteries left it last
night. Nothing done. Our guns all silent & the enemy
pegging away as usual every ten minutes from James
Island. thus endeth the second lesson. It was
cold as Greenland at sunrise — Overcoats are
not uncomfortable — but if they were we should not suffer
for there isn't one in the regiment

Admiral Fanagut had come down. Somebody's come. I should say for the monitors are really fighting for the first time since I've been here – How I wish you were here dear Frankie – It's bright moonlight – clear & cold, so cold that I got numb in my lookout & had to come down to warm. The deep round crash of our big guns is tremendous. Just think – 2 batteries of 200 pds one 300 pd. Six monitors with 15 inch guns & old Ironsides with her huge battery all flashing & roaring away like mad. The enemies fire was incessant At first – but has mainly dried up – I think somebody is hurt. Shall hope to see a bigger hole in Sumpter than ever before. Shouldn't wonder if soldiers are wanted in the morning for some storming.

Sumpter has not fired a gun. It is done up from this campaign. Ive seen a good deal of powder burned – but I never heard anything so grand as the roll of those monster guns.

2 A.M Sept 2nd    Have been found & stirred up all my Camp guard in case the enemy should make a dash at daylight on Folly Island while the gun boats are Busy in Light House inlet. Don't know as I can do any more. So laying out round & revolver handy – I'll soon have a nap spite of the guns.

9 A.M.    Was out at sunrise & in my lookout to see what was up. Alas, nothing – as usual. I've scanned Camp work. Sumpter is as the land batteries left it last night. Nothing done. Our guns all silent & the enemy pegging away as usual every ten minutes from James Island. Thus endeth the second lesson. It was cold as Greenland at sunrise. Our coats are not uncomfortable – but if they were we should not suffer for there isn't one in the regiment.    (cont.)

9 P.M. Sept 2nd. This scrawl must be closed and
mailed — It has been written in scraps — but is
The best I can do — There is something about
This S.C. campaign which is singularly depressing
and even when having an hours leisure it seems
impossible to do anything but lie down & study old
advertisements in antiquated papers. There be
So many possibilities between this & our next
meeting that I hardly form conception of it — Only
I know that it would be a bright hour were you
by my side now & it will be bright when that
hour comes. Had we remained at New
Berne — I think you might have spent the winter
there or at Roanoke pleasantly & happily. How
much we should be together would depend on the
activity of our campaigning — Gen Wild still claims
that we are to return in course of six or eight weeks
but I've seen too much of Military humbuggery to have
the slightest hope. Unless greater energy is shown than
now appears. My judgment as to taking Charleston
by November even will prove incorrect and there is
No reason to hope that we shall be suffered to leave
the department until Charleston is taken or the Campaign
abandoned. One event is perhaps as likely as the other
    If by any chance we should happen to return before
Novr — I don't know of a pleasanter place for you.

9 P.M. Sept. 2nd     This scrawl must be closed and mailed – it has been written in scraps – but is the best I can do. There is something about this S.C. Campaign which is singularly depressing and even when having an hours leisure it seems impossible to do anything but lie down & study old advertisements in antiquated papers. There lie so many possibilities between this & our next meeting that I hardly form conception of it – only I know that it would be a bright hour were you by my side now & it will be bright when that hour comes. Had we remained at New Berne – I think you might have spent the winter there or at Roanoke pleasantly & happily. How much we should be together would depend on the activity of our campaigning. Gen Wild still claims that we are to return in course of six or eight weeks but I've seen too much of Military humbuggery to have the slightest hope. Unless greater energy is shown than now appears. My judgment as to taking Charleston by November even will prove incorrect and there is no reason to hope that we shall be suffered to leave the department until Charleston is taken or the Campaign abandoned. One event is perhaps as likely as the other.

If by any chance we should happen to return before Nov. I don't know of a pleasanter place for your     (*cont.*)

wintering. However if we plan nothing we run less risk of disappointment. I have written two or three letters to brother John Hooker. about a note of mine due Sept 17th which I had provided for in event of being at New Berne in last of August but which is all unprovided for in our breaking up. I have enough due me to pay the note twice over but our pay rolls are all at New Berne & I have no hope of pay until we can 1st get the Rolls - 2nd find a paymaster. 3rd the Paymaster get the money There is no present prospect of any one of the three being accomplished. I have written asking to have the note renewed &c. Hope some one of my letters has gotten safely through. I wrote you a line at starting from New. Berne. Another from Hilton Head and a third from Folly Island on landing. Have written twice since. So this makes No 4 from Folly Island.

I am anxious for later news than came in the last batch from New Berne. which only came to Augt 22d We find letters on this sand bank hugely - Stamps are hard to find others nearly out - have plenty in My desk at New Berne - Write often as you can I can read if I cannot write

Lovingly ever truly yrs
J Crtb

wintering. However if we plan nothing we run less risk of disappointment. I have written two or three letters to brother John Hooker about a note of mine due Sept 4th/7th which I had provided for in event of being at New Berne in last of August but which is all unprovided for in our breaking up I have enough I'm one to pay the note twice over But out pay rolls are all at New Berne & I have No hope of pay until we can 1st Get the rolls – 2nd find a paymaster. 3d the Paymaster get the money. There is no present prospect of any one of the three being accomplished – I have written asking to have the note received etc. Hope some one of my letters has gotten safely through. I wrote you a line at starting from New Berne. Another from Hilton Head. and a third from Folly Island on landing. Have written twice since. So this makes No 4 from Folly Island.

I'm anxious for later news than came in the last batch from New Berne – which only came 12 Aug. We need letters on this sand bank hugely – stamps are hard to find & I'm nearly out. Have plenty in my desk at New Berne. Write often as you can I can read if I cannot write –

Lovingly ever truly yrs

J C B

Copy-

Head quarters 3d Brigade
Folly Island S. C. Jan'y 13th 1864

Hon Henry Wilson -
　　　Sir

　　　　　I have the honor to forward a few State-
ments respecting a regiment of Colored troops raised
and commanded by me, hoping that they may
possibly be of service.

　　　　　The first Enlistment in my Command was
at New Berne N. C. May 28th 1863; the regiment was fully
organized, uniformed, armed & equipped by 26th June
and was mustered into service on the 30th. From 30th
June to 31st July the regiment was on active duty in
and about New Berne, and acquired considerable
proficiency of drill.

　　　　　On 31st July I embarked the Command for Charleston, where it arrived safely on 3d August, in the
Afternoon, and at 6.30 A.M. of the 4th, the whole available force was detailed to the trenches on Morris
Island elsewhere. From that date to 1st December
I can safely say that I never saw my command
together. The details for fatigue absorbing ~~continually~~

The whole available force with scarcely an intermission
So that it was with the utmost difficulty that I was
able to preserve anything like a Soldierly organization

This abuse has now passed away and
I am encouraged to believe that when all facts
are considered, these Colored troops will be found
fully worthy of any favor which has been or may
extended. In this belief I respectfully represent as
follows.

1. My Command was enlisted (in accordance
with the legal interpretation given to the Act of Congress)
for ten dollars per Month, three dollars of which to
be in clothing. They were assured however that ultimately they should receive the same pay with White
Troops. _They relied on this_, not merely in
a money point of view but in the wider sense of
_Soldierly equality_. and I sincerely believe that
confidence in this and hope of it and ambition
for it have done more than any one thing
to make them diligent & patient & anxious for
improvement. They have determined to
deserve equality and I do most earnestly testify
that they have deserved and do now deserve it.

The damage of inferior pay is that it

becomes a constant reminder to the men that they are held to be inferior, of necessity. Whereby one great incentive & encouragement to duty — is lost.

2.      The constant hard work imposed on my Command has caused extra wear and tear of clothing.

Their work has been largely in the Salt Marshes of these islands, in water and mud — also at the various landings loading & unloading cargoes. And the consequence is that with the utmost care on my part, the yearly allowance for clothing was in most cases exceeded in the first five months. At this date the average clothing account of each man is about fifty one dollars ($51.00) So that after seven months constant fatigue of the toughest kind & often under heavy fire — there is apparently but about $17.00 now due — and as the men were paid off at $7.00 per month, to 31st October they are really in debt to the government at the close of 1863 in sufficient amount to absorb their pay for two months to come. Is it requiring too much to ask that their back pay be granted them? or at least an extra allowance of clothing?

3d      A large number of my men have wives and children in North Carolina within our

Jan 13

lines and dependant on them for Support.

From many letters which have been brought to my notice, I learn that the women & children in many instances have suffered not a little in absence of husbands and fathers. My men have richly earned full pay. Can it not be Secured to them for the months that have passed?

4. Government is now indebted to my Command to the amount of ($30.000. ov) thirty thousand dollars nearly for work done previous to enlistment — many of the men having been at work from six to ten months without pay. In absence of vouchers, it is doubtful whether any of this fairly earned amount can be collected. and Surely, in view of this loss suffered by them as "Contrabands", they are entitled to prompt con-Sideration as "Soldiers."

In addition to the forgoing, I have only to add my personal testimony to the general good conduct of my men. They are good Soldiers & become more & more manly every day. Every thing done by Government showing that they are held in an equally with white troops, is quickly known & most fully appreciated. With sincere respect — I am

Yours Very truly

Ja.C. Beecher. Col 1st N. C. Col'd Vols.

Hd qrs 1st N.C.C. Vols
Jacksonville Fla
Mch 14th 1864

My dearest –

Mr "Christian Commission man" says a letter will go tonight in time for mail. I write a line to let you of work and contentment except as I long for you.

I was Gen Off of the day yesterday, & inspected the picket line. There is no enemy within four or five miles of my immediate front. There are said to be some on line of Rail Road. I sketched the semi circle found by our forces. This is my position. I think we shall fight soon at Baldwin. where the enemy are intrenching.

I hope the guns for my Regt

will not be delayed.

My men fought that fight with guns that the other Regiments would not have gone into action with. It is a shame that good men cant have good guns—

Frankie dear. Ive lost that little photograph which I pocketed at Lunnford. Imiss it ever so much. Wont you send me a "pictur". To make me feel as though my tent were shared by you—

17th Ive so many things to do that I dont know which to do at first. Am glad I hurried on.

Belle went in Cosmopolitan on 14th I wanted to go early yet didnt want to either—

I like my boys right well. Gen Seymour was

taken aback by the enemy fighting
behind trees. So four or five Reg'ts
are picked out to drive in Indian
fashion. Mine is one. You
would think us more perfectly
mad, to see us dashing through
the woods. Yelling & dodging & ...
from behind logs & all sorts of things
    I'm afraid Kenny will forget the
guns at Washington. Let our
two months pay to have them
here now.

    Everything is quiet yet.
You wouldn't suppose an
enemy within 100 miles.
My Major is probably alive.
All goes well in the Command
    If we should not be before
the enemy in May. I think
I can get leave so as to spend
three or four days at home.
Will try to do so. How I long
for those days.

I'll write longer articles when
I have more time. It's
time I heard from you.
Don't delay the photograph
for I am truly without sight
of you.
Lovingly yours
Jas. C. B.

Officers Hosp Ward. 6
    Beaufort S. C. Dec 2nd 64

My beloved.
            I'm grateful for life spared
though very sorrowful at being on my back.
    We had a hard fight under great
disadvantage.      There was only one
road. with thick jungle on either side
& the enemy had 2 guns right sweeping
the road.    I was 5th Regt. & was ordered
up. to move through the thicket along the
right of the road. flank the battery, and
charge it.    I did so. but the enemy
ran the guns off. & I came right in
front of a strong earth work that
nobody knew anything about. A round
shot killed poor old Gray. I left
him & pushed on at head of my column
A round shot struck me across both
legs above the knee & upset me. I
found no bone broken & pushed on

Officers Hosp. Ward 6

Beaufort, S.C., Dec. 2nd '64

My beloved,

I'm grateful for life spared though very sorrowful at being on my back.

We had a hard fight under great disadvantage. There was only one road, with thick jungle on either side & the enemy had 2 guns right sweeping the road. I was 5th Regt. & was ordered up, to move through the thicket along the right of the road, flank the battery and charge it. I did so, but the enemy ran the guns off, & I came right in front of a strong earth work that nobody knew anything about. A round shot killed poor old Gray. I left him & pushed on at head of my column a round shot struck me across both legs above the knee & upset me. I found no bone broken & pushed on.     (*cont.*)

then the boys opened fire without
orders. and the bushes were so
thick that the companies were
getting mixed. I halted and
reformed the companies. then
got orders to move to left of the
earth work & try to carry it.
I led off by the left flank, the
boys starting finely singing out
"follow the Colonel". ~~When I for~~
It was a perfect jungle all laced
with grape vines. when I got on
the left of the earth work, and
closed up I found that another
regiment had marched right through
mine & cut it off. So that I only
had about 20 men. We could
see the rebel gunners loading. I told
the boys to fire on them & raise a
yell. hoping to make them think
I had a force on their flank. We
fired & shouted & got a volley or two
in return. A rascally bullet

Then the boys opened fire without orders, and the bushes were so thick that the companies were getting mixed. I halted and reformed the companies. Then got orders to move to left of the earth work & try to carry it.

I led off by the left flank, the boys starting finely & crying out "follow de cunnel." It was a perfect jungle all laced with grape vines, & when I got on the left of the earth work and closed up, I found that another regiment had marched right through mine & cut it off, so that I only had about 20 men. We could see the rebel gunners loading. I told the boys to fire on them & raise a yell, hoping to make them think I had a force on their flank. We fired and shouted & got a volley or two in return. A rascally bullet

(*cont.*)

hit me just below the groin ranged
down nearly through my thigh. Then
I went back with my twenty to the
road again. found 38th 53d 54th men
all mixed together. Went to work to
clean up — though the fire of the
enemy was very hot. Got hit here
with a spent ball a left hand.
In course of an hour got the corn.
[illegible] all right in order.

Tony cleared at dark and
held our ground. I was so
stiff that I couldn't get along. *
~~[illegible] [illegible] [illegible]~~ So
I shook hand with Col Williams who
did splendidly all day wasn't touched
and Lee Murray helped me back to the
Branch — then I was sent to the
boat. Here I am. Stiff and helpless
but not dangerously hurt. only grieving
that I couldn't take the battery. I
would have done it if they hadn't
torn it off. and I would have

hit me just below the groin & ranged down nearly through my thigh. Then I went back with my twenty to the road again, found the 35th, 55th, 54th men all mixed together. Went to work to clean-up, though the fire of the enemy was very hot. Got hit here with a spent ball in left hand. In course of an hour got the companies all right & in order.

Firing ceased at dark, we held our ground. I was so dizzy that I couldn't get along so I shook hands with Col. Willard who did splendidly all day and wasn't touched and Dr. Marcy helped me back the church, then I was sent to the boat & here I am. Stiff and helpless but not dangerously hurt, only grieving that I couldn't take the battery. I would have     *(cont.)*

had the earth work if I had
had 300 men instead of 20.

I dont murmur. But I would
be very grateful to God if I might
have done it even though I hadnt
come back from it — for no advance
can be made without taking it.
The force has suffered a good deal
all regiments losing officers especially
Comd's officers. Col. Hartwell of 55th
Mass is wounded — I hear Col Lewis
is also. but dont know certainly
We were about 4 miles from
R. Road. I could hear the
cars coming with reinforcements.
Then the Rebs would yell
& howl — Decr 3d. Cant learn
much from the front. It is
reported that the enemy have
abandoned the battery —

Im pretty blue & helpless but
in less pain when quiet. The
54th & 3-5th undertook to charge

done it if they hadn't run it off and I would have had the earth work

if I had 300 men instead of 20.

I don't murmur but I would be very grateful to God if I

might have done it even though I hadn't come back from it, for no

advance can be made without taking it. The force suffered a good

deal all regiments losing officers especially Comm. Officers. Col.

Hartwell of 55th Mass. is wounded, I hear Col. Lewis is also, but

don't know certainly. We were about 4 miles from R. Road, & could

hear the guns coming with enforcements.

Then the Rebs would yell and howl.

Dec. 3d Can't learn much from the front. It is reported that the

enemy have abandoned the battery.

I'm pretty blue and helpless but in less pain when quiet. The

54th & 55th undertook to charge     *(cont.)*

The earth work and were driven back. Thats what mixed them all up with my men.

I am going to try to be sent to Jacksonville as soon as I can be moved. You had better remain until hearing again from me.

Dont be worried, dearest. It will all come out right by and by.

The surgeon is going to try for the ball in my right thigh today. I will probably find it. At all events it will not do harm beyond crippling me for a month or so. Give my love to Mrs Willard. Say that the Lt Col is unhurt. & is in Command.

God bless my beloved wife.

I only know of Capt White & Lt Krebs wounded

Lovingly your husband

J. C. Beecher

I cant hear anything from my "Kate" but hope she is alive & safe the earth work and were driven back. That's what mixed them all up with my men.

I am going to try to be sent to Jacksonville as soon as I can be moved. You had better remain until hearing again from me. Don't be worried dearest it will all come out right by and by.

The surgeon is going to try for the ball in my right thigh today & will probably find it. At all events it will not do harm beyond limping now for a month or so. Give my love to Mrs. Willard. Say that the Lt. Col. is unhurt & is in command.

God bless my beloved wife

I only know of Capt. White & Lt. Kolb wounded.

Lovingly your husband

J. C. Beecher

I can't hear anything from my "Kate" (his other horse) but hope she is alive & safe.

Off Hosp dec¹ᵘᵗʰ.

On his back.

What become of

my wife?

James ✝ Beecher
mark

New York, 34 Pine St
Dec 16. 1864

Rev. Henry Ward Beecher
                    Dear Sir

                              Knowing how anxious you
must feel to hear from your brother (Col. B.), I hasten
to send you such information as has come to me —

          My son in law A. J. Willard is his Lieut. Col.
and I received letters from my daughter yesterday,
dated at Jacksonville, Fla, the 6th instant. She writes
that orders came on the 25th ult. for some five or six
Regiments there to leave immediately for further west.
And they did leave accordingly on the 27th — Your brother
had charge of the whole force as Brig. Genl.; ~~having~~ and
Willard took command of the Reg.t —

                              For some ten days no steamer
arrived at Jacksonville — Mrs. Beecher & Mrs. Willard the
only ladies there — all the troops gone except
the small force left to garrison the fort — The Chaplin
him the only one left behind to care for the ladies.
They continued in ignorance of all that was transpiring
until the 5th Dec — when a steamer arrived bringing
intelligence of the battle and skirmishes which
had occurred — Col. Beecher was reported to have

distinguished himself by his bravery, and to have been
dangerously wounded — But he wrote to his wife that
it was <u>not</u> so — It was true he had received three
distinct wounds (one in his left thigh) and was
being taken to the hospital at Beaufort; & requested
his wife to come immediately on to him — He wrote
M<sup>rs</sup> B. that the col<sup>ds</sup> troops, and particularly his own
Regiment behaved nobly — never broke nor flinch:
— My daughter says your brother is idolized by the
men, — and that there is not a man in the Re
giment who would not sacrifice his life for him

M<sup>rs</sup> Becker was to leave Jacksonville on the 7<sup>th</sup>
to join her husband —

I am, Sir,
Yours Truly
L. Platt

Hd grs 38th N.J.C.T. 1st Bry
Bivouac 1 mile from Combahee ferry.
Sunday Feby 19th 1865.

Dearest.

I got to rest yesterday at 10
AM. found every man in ranks - all
ready. Such Cheering! It did me
good. Officers then all came in
+ seemed most cordial - Had all
I could do shaking hands with
everybody - Had service at 10 Am.
Waiting for rations - along with 107 N.Y.
Moved 20th Inches at day light.
having got 5 ds rations last night.
Passed 2nd Brigade at Ashepoo
bridge. Caught the rest of the
1st Brigade at Edisto river at 11. v.
Bridge burned. While Engineers are
at work repairing. I am ordered to take
by right of 107 N.Y. across in the RR.
Have also burned for 5 ds yet in

middle of river. Trestle high
1 mile long. Crosser burnt part.
Single planks. Single file — then walked
on stringers & sleepers 1/2 mile, dead &
leave horses behind. Got safe
across, & pushed along six miles
Camped for night. My leg growling
but serviceable yet. All tell you
of our Campings. raidings & burnings when
I come back.

Tuesday — Marched 8 miles & hallted
for artillery. 1.30 P.M rear of Brigade
Came up. I led off in advance
until 4 P.M when rear of Brigade
hallted. and I was ordered to push
on with 88th U.S. & 107 N.Y. to Wallace
& Railroad bridges, (both reported burned)
look out for the enemy & repair bridges.
Marched till dark & camped 4
miles from bridge. My horses have
come up — & two stolen horses more
captured
also wagons & carts. so am well
off for Chickens & transportation.

Wednesday - 7 A.m. reached Wallaces bridge. found it smoking - but not burned enough to hurt it. Pushed across with advance guard. found large earth work. 3 guns 32 pounders in good order. one loaded with canister. Sent a scout on 1 mile to Rantoul bridge - Burned all up. Ordered forward the column across Wallaces bridge. Stacked arms. manned the fort and set to work to repair Rantoul bridge. Sent scouts partly up the river. worked on bridge for 4 hours. Scouts partly came back reporting better bridge 2½ miles up stream. Reported it to Col Van Wyck. Capt Bryant. who had just come up. Rode up with him & inspected bridge. Concluded it was best one. Rode back & ordered up the column. Went to work on bridge & finished it by 4 P.m. and rode over

Came back to camp. Thoroughly tired out. Have been in saddle since from 6 A.M. to 6 P.M. and no dinner. Have splendid supper of Chickens & sweet potatoes. Feel better — but lame.

We have skinned the country thus far. It grieves one to see such splendid horses and furniture burnt up. But we cant take it along. and up they go. Tonight the whole horizon is lighted up splendidly. No less than four grand Conflagrations going on at once.

I shall get to be a regular brigand. We are only 10 miles from Charleston. but I dont think we will go there. Probably will have to scour this district for some days. Have seen no regular troops. Am occasionally fired on by bush whackers. Nancy is well. invaluable to me. Tonight I have 20 horses & oxen. / two horse carriage &c. &c. and Chickens enough to stock a farm yard.

D.M. Terry & Dr Mackey are the
best leaders for cavalry parties I
have. Personally I have only stolen
3 horses. one cart and a
Methodist minister – who begged
hard for the horses, but I told
him he & his brother ministers by
their preaching – have forced me
to leave the pulpit & take to fighting
and do not only take his horses
but burn his house if it came
on my line of march.

     D. M. Terry goes to Charleston
for rations tomorrow – so I send
my Memo. along.

     I love you Frankie dear – While
burning houses. or stealing horses. & very
pretty piece of furniture that goes
to ashes. reminds me how I wish
it was in our house – These planters
have lived most luxuriously – but
they have got to rough it now.

     When I shall be tomorrow night
I don't know – but wherever

it is I shall wind up my days
means for my wife - & then lie down
in my blanket. & pray for God's
blessing on her

Col Williams is well. He is
bridge builder in chief

Lovingly ever
Your affectionate
J. C. B.

Riverside. March 24.

1885.

My own dear husband,

Sister Belle is so kind as to write me nearly every day how she thinks you are, but I was very glad to hear from you in your own handwriting. In reply to what you say of a little house & living by ourselves I would gladly please you rather than myself, of course, & if you were well, you would only have to choose the place & say, "come" & I should go, as I always have. But as it is, I hope you will try to be satisfied with what I do, knowing that I do not take a step without prayer & advice & using my own brains, & then whatever happens, it must be the right thing, because I do the very best I know, & whatever comes we must receive as being the very best thing that could happen to us, because our Father loves us & cares for every hair of our heads. And surely he will over-rule all our

mistakes even for our good. I tried
to get Uncle Nelson's cottage, as I told
you, but failed & you said you were glad,
for you could not have stood it, and I
know of no other except that little tenement
house of Mr. Martin's, & that you would
not like any better. It would not do
to throw up my means of support until
you are prepared to take care of us, for
if I disperse my children boarders, I might
not be able to get them again when I
wanted them. And then on your account,
has not a quiet place of late simply
meant, freedom to pursue the train of
thought which so injures you? Do you
not need for your health, association
with your kind, & conversation &c?

At any rate, after taking three months
for consideration, I found I could do
no better than continue here another year,
& after I gave the decision the other day,
I cannot now draw back. Therefore I en-
treat of you to look at the pleasant things
you can do & make the best of the place,
for my sake & all our sakes. In haste your Frankie

Riverside March 30th 85.

My own beloved

Your letter of
Saturday night is such a precious
one to your little wife — so full of
trust & love — no husband can
be a sweeter & better lover than
you are. And it makes me
long all the more for you to be
well enough to take your place at
my side, & at the head of our
little establishment. You speak
of coming right home, & I am
sure nothing could delight
me more — if the Doctor
says he has done you all
the good he can. But why
do you allow yourself to
be so impatient of everything
you try? You know that a
three yrs. illness like yours
cannot be cured in a week's
time. Why not then say

Riverside March 30, 1885

My own beloved,

Your letter of Saturday night is such a precious one to your little wife - so full of trust & love - no husband can be a sweeter & better lover than you are. And it makes me long all the more, for you to be well enough to take your place at my side, & at the head of our little establishment. You speak of coming right home, and I am sure nothing could delight me more - if the Doctor says he has done you all the good he can. But why do you allow yourself to be so impatient of everything you try? You knew that a three yrs. illness like yours cannot be cured in a week's time. Why not then

say      (*cont.*)

to the Doctor — "how long do you want me to stay with you?" "Shall I promise to give you a month? no doctor in the world could help a patient who is pulling away from him all the time as you do from Dr. W. If he does not cure you, he will certainly say you would not let him. Remember he is the only one who says he can cure you. So, much as I want to see your dear face, I will not by my impatience spoil the effect of all we have gone through in going to Boston & staying there. They have more means of cure there than any where else. Don't come away until you are cured.

Tell Mrs. Walling I have

to the doctor - "how long do you want me to stay with you?" "Shall

I promise to give you a month"? No doctor in the world could help

a patient who is pulling away from him all the time as you co from

Dr. W. If he does not cure you, he will certainly say you would not

let him. Remember he is the only one who says he can cure you. So,

much as I want to see your dear face, I will not by my impatience

spoil the effect of all we have gone through in going to Boston &

staying there.

They have more means of care there than anywhere else.

Don't come away until you are cured.

Tell Mrs. Walling I have     (*cont.*)

just heard through my music teacher of a cure made by her friend Mrs. Stuart that is wonderful. Perhaps she could add the mind cure to what is now being done.

But any way, do give all your expectation & patient waiting, & cooperation to your kind old Dr. W.

Don't give up the ship—say you will get well. Pray for it, expect it.

Sister Belle will tell you of our visit together. I listened with all docility on Sunday aft. and evening to see if the spiritualists could tell me anything that would do me good—but I found nothing that added to my previous faith in the dear Savior & Friend, who ever leadeth us—nothing to draw me from just heard through my music teacher of a cure made by her friend

Mrs. Stuart that is wonderful. Perhaps she could add the mind cure

to what is now being done.

But any way, do give all your expectation & patient waiting

& cooperation to your kind old Dr. W.

Don't give up the ship - say you <u>will</u> get well. <u>Pray</u> for it,

<u>expect</u> it.

Sister Belle will tell you of our visit together. I listened with

all docility on Sunday aft. and evening to see if the spiritualists

could tell me anything that would do me good - but I found nothing

that added to my previous faith in the dear Savior & Friend, who

ever leadeth us - nothing to draw me from  *(cont.)*

my own Church. I wish
you would go every Sunday to
Philips Brooks church, & sit
where you can hear well,
& go to the communion whenever they have it — which of
course will be next Sunday
which is the Blessed Easter — oh
let us rise from our dead
past & Christ will give us
light. Sister Mary will go
with you, & be delighted to have
you ask her to. Write & tell
me that you have.

now do be a good boy &
think of nothing, nothing
but how to get well.

I am having a bad cold
but it is better than yesterday
Your own devoted
Frankie

my own church. I wish you would go every Sunday to Philips Brooks

church, & sit where you can hear well, and go to the communion

whenever they have it - Which of course will be next Sunday which

is the blessed Easter - oh let us rise from our dead past & Christ

will give us light. Sister Mary will go with you, & be <u>delighted</u> to

have you ask her to. Write & tell me that you have.

Now do be a good boy & think of nothing, <u>nothing</u> but how

to get well.

I am having a bad cold but it is better than yesterday.

Your very devoted

Frankie

# *Bibliography*

Allman, T. D. *Finding Florida: The True History of the Sunshine State*. New York: Atlantic Monthly Press, 2013.

American Battlefield Trust. "Answers to Your Civil War Questions." Online at https://www.civilwar.org?education/history/faq.

———."Fort Wagner Battlefield." Online at https://www.battlefields.org/visit/battlefields/fort-wagner-battlefield.

———."Malvern Hill Battlefield." Online at https://www.battlefields.org/visit/battlefields/malvern-hill-battlefield.

Ball, Edward. "Slavery's Enduring Resonance." *New York Times*, March 14, 2015: SR5.

———.Slaves in the Family, Ballantine Book Publishing, 1998.

Barrus, Clara. *The Life and Letters of John Burroughs*, 2 vols. New York: Russell & Russell, 1925.

Beecher-Stowe family papers, 1798-1956: A Finding Aid. Radcliff Institute for Advanced Study, Harvard University, Cambridge, MA. Online at https://hollisarchives.lib.harvard.edu/repositories/8/resources/4857.

Bonney, Catharina V. R. *A Legacy of Historical Gleanings*, 2 vols. Albany, New York: J. Munsell, 1875.

Burroughs, John. "Birch Browsings." *Atlantic Monthly*, July 1869.

*Christian Recorder, The*. "Presentation of a Flag." published by the African Methodist Episcopal Church. Philadelphia, Pennsylvania, November 21, 1863.

*Christian Union, The*. Edited by Henry Ward Beecher & Lyman Abbott. New York: New York & Brooklyn Publishing Co., 1870-1935.

Emilio, Louis F. *A Brave Black Regiment: History of the Fifty-Fourth Regiment of Massachusetts Volunteers 1863-1865*. Boston: The Boston Book Company, 1894.

Glenn, Myra C. Thomas K. Beecher: *Minister to a Changing America 1824-1900*. Westport, CT: Greenwood Press, 1996.

Hallowell, N. P. *Letter to Boston Transcript*, quoted in Booker T. Washington, *The Story of the Negro*, 2 vols. New York: Doubleday Page & Co., 1909.

Halston. "Some Hit and Miss Chat." *New York Times*, August 27, 1886: 2.

*Harper's Weekly*, "Treatment of Captured Colored Soldiers." August 15, 1863.

*Hartford Evening Press*, March 5, 1864, republished in *New England Loyal Publication Society*, March 19, 1864.

Hedrick, Joan D. *Harriet Beecher Stowe*. New York: Oxford University Press, 1994.

Helmuth, William Todd. *A System of Surgery*. New York: Boericke & Tafil, 1879.

Horstman, Jonathan W. "The African-American's Civil War: A History of the 1st North Carolina Colored Volunteers." M.A. thesis, Western Carolina University, 1994. Online at https://www.ncgenweb.us/ncusct/1stnccv.htm.

Horwitz, Tony. "Did Civil War Soldiers have PTSD?" *Smithsonian Magazine*, January 2015.

Hutchins, Shana Renee. "Just learning to be Men: A History of the 35th United States Colored Troops 1863-1866." M.A. thesis, North Carolina State University, 1999.

James Chaplin Beecher Papers, A-123, folder #1-58. Schlesinger Library, Radcliffe Institute, Harvard University, Cambridge, MA.

Judd, David W. "Beecher's Clearing." *American Agriculturist*, September 1881.

Knox, Thomas. *Life and Work of Henry Ward Beecher*. Hartford: Park Publishing Co., 1887.

Low, Charles P. *Some Recollections by Captain Charles P. Low*. Boston: Geo. H. Ellis Co., 1906.

Olajide, Olayanju. *The Complete Concise History of the Slave Trade*. Bloomington, Indiana: Author House, 2013.

Perkins, Frances Beecher. "A Seven Years Outing." *New England Magazine*, July 1900.

Perkins, Frances Beecher. "Two Years with a Colored Regiment." *New England Magazine*, January 1898.

Plumley, Ladd. *With the Trout Fly*. New York: Fredrick A. Stokes, 1929.

Pohanka, Brian C. "Fort Wagner and the 54th Massachusetts Volunteer Infantry." *America's Civil War Magazine*, September 1991.

Reid, Richard. "Raising the African Brigade: Early Black Recruitment in Civil War North Carolina." *North Carolina Historical Review* 70, no. 3, July 1993.

Rugoff, Milton. *The Beechers: An American Family in the Nineteenth Century*. New York: Harper & Row Publishers, 1981.

*Sailor's Magazine, The*. New York: American Seamen's Friend Society, 1837-1864.

*Semi-Weekly Louisianian*. "First reunion of the Officers of the Thirty-fifth Regiment United States Colored Troops." December 10, 1871, reprinted from *The Grand Army Journal*.

Singleton, Robert R. "James C. Beecher and the Freedmen's Bureau." *Mississippi Quarterly* 53, No. 1, 1999.

*Soldiers and Patriots Biographical Album*. Chicago: Union Veteran Pub. Co., 1892.

Stowe, Lyman Beecher. *Saints, Sinners and Beechers*. Indianapolis: Bobbs-Merrill Co., 1934.

Trudeau, Noah Andre. *Like Men of War: Black Troops in the Civil War 1862-1865*. Boston: Little, Brown and Co., 1998.

*The Union Army: A History of Military Affairs in the Loyal States 1861-65* vol. 6. Madison, Wisconsin: Federal Pub. Co., 1908.

Washington, Booker T. *The Story of the Negro*. New York: Doubleday Page & Co., 1909.

White, Barbara. *The Beecher Sisters*. New Haven: Yale University Press, 2003.

Williams, George W. *A History of the Negro Troops in the War of the Rebellion 1861-1865*. New York: Harper & Bros. 1888.

# Illustration Credits

Historical images and illustrations have been digitally retouched to remove dust, scratches, and other visual imperfections for the highest quality reproduction.

*i*      Van Put, Lee, photographer. "Beecher Lake." Photograph. Livingston Manor: Lee Van Put, c2020.

*ii*     Harding, Arthur Robert. *Science of fishing: the most practical book on fishing ever published.* Illustration. Columbus, Ohio: A. R. Harding, 1912.

*iv*    Wilson, D.W., photographer. "[Portrait of James Beecher in military uniform.]" Photograph. Hartford, Connecticut, ca. 1861-1865. Schlesinger Library on the History of Women in America, Radcliffe Institute, Beecher-Stowe family papers, 1798-1956 (hereafter BSFP). http://id.lib.harvard.edu/via/olvwork20018362/catalog

*ix*    Harris, William C., editor. *The American Angler.* Illustration. February 1899, Vol. 29, 60.

*xii*   United States Geological Survey. *Ulster County, New York.* Map. https://gis.orangecountygov.com/orange/

*8*      Van Put, Lee, photographer. "Approaching Beecher Lake." Photograph. Livingston Manor: Lee Van Put, c2020.

11  Van Put, Lee, photographer. "Overlooking Beecher Lake." Photograph. Livingston Manor: Lee Van Put, c2020.

16  Rhead, Louis. *The Speckled Brook Trout*. Illustration. New York: R. H. Russell, 1902.

18  Low, Charles Porter. *Some Recollections by Captain Charles P. Low*. Illustration. Boston: Geo. H. Ellis co., 1905.

22  Allom, Thomas. *The Chinese Empire, Illustrated*. Painting. London: London Printing and Publishing Company, 1858.

26  Ashley, Clifford W., artist. *Whaleships of New Bedford: Sixty plates from drawings by Clifford W. Ashley*. Illustration. Boston: Houghton Mifflin Company, 1929.

29  De Lamater, R.S., photographer. "[Portrait of James Beecher.]" Photograph. Hartford, Connecticut, ca. 1861-1866. BSFP.

33  Chappel, Alonso, artist. *Battle of Fair Oaks. Gallant Charge of Gen Casey's Division to Save the Guns*. Painting. New York: Johnson Fry & Co., c1862.

36  Mead, Larkin, artist. Charge of General Sickles's Brigade Upon the Rebels at the Battle of Fairoaks. Illustration. *Harper's Weekly*, June 21, 1862, 392-393.

40  Homer, Winslow, artist. Our Outlying Picket in the Woods. Illustration. *Harper's Weekly*, June 7, 1862, 359

42  Chappel, Alonso, artist. *Battle of Malvern Hill*. Painting. New York: Alonzo Chappel, 1862.

45  Cook, George, photographer. "[Portrait of James Beecher in military uniform.]" Photograph. Charleston, South Carolina, ca. 1864-1866. BSFP.

49  The Late Colonel Robert G. Shaw. Illustration. *Harper's Weekly*, August 15, 1863, 525

51  The Escaped Slave in the Union Army. Illustration. *Harper's Weekly*, July 2, 1864, 428

53    "[Colored infantry camp.]" Photograph. ca. 1861-1869. From Library of
      Congress; Selected Civil War Photographs, 1861-1865 (hereafter LOC).
      https://www.loc.gov/pictures/item/2018670907/

55    Brady, Mathew B, photographer. "[1st U.S. colored infantry.]"
      Photograph. ca. 1861-1869. LOC.
      https://www.loc.gov/pictures/item/2004673345/

58    "[Negro Soldiers, South Carolina.]" Photograph. ca. 1861-1869. LOC.
      https://www.loc.gov/pictures/item/2013647889/

62    Haas & Peale, photographer. "[Morris Island, South Carolina.
      Unidentified camp.]" Photograph. c1863. LOC.
      https://www.loc.gov/pictures/item/2018667757/

65    The Late Brigadier-General George C. Strong. Illustration. *Harper's
      Weekly*, August 15, 1863, 525.

68    Kurz & Allison. *Storming Fort Wagner*. South Carolina United States
      Fort Wagner Morris Island, ca. 1890. Painting. Chicago: Kurz &
      Allison-Art Publishers, c1890. https://www.loc.gov/item/2012647346/

70    Nash, Thomas, artist. *Attack on Fort Wagner*. Painting. c1863. New
      York Public Library Digital Collections. https://digitalcollections.nypl.
      org/items/510d47e0-fa01-a3d9-e040-e00a18064a99

71    "[New rifle musket ball caliber 58-inch.]" Illustration. 1855.
      Smithsonian Neg. No. 91-10712; Harpers Ferry NHP Cat. No. 13645.
      https://www.nps.gov/media/photo/view.
      htm?id=29A9A32D-1DD8-B71C-078B7F65E6877131

77    "[Camp on Morris Island]" Photograph. ca. 1861-1865. LOC.
      https://www.loc.gov/item/2014646422/

78    Russell, Andrew J., photographer. "[Building stockade, Alexandria,
      Va.]" Photograph. Alexandria, Virginia, ca. 1861-1865. LOC.
      https://www.loc.gov/item/2014645754/

83    Barber's House at the Ford on Big Creek, Colonel Barton's
      Headquarters. Illustration. *Harper's Weekly*, March 12, 1864, 172.

85    Kurz and Allison. *Battle of Olustee*. Color lithography. 1894.
      Metropolitan Museum of Art, New York.
      https://www.metmuseum.org/art/collection/search/388625

87    Cooley, Sam A., photographer. "[Portrait of James Beecher in military uniform.]" Photograph. Folly Island, Couth Carolina, c1863. BSFP.

89    Vail Brothers, photographer. "[Portrait of an unidentified woman.]" Photograph. Poughkeepsie, ca. 1858-1866. BSFP.

92    Wilson, D.W., photographer. "[Portrait of James Beecher and his wife, Frances]" Photograph. Hartford, Connecticut, ca. 1864-1866. BSFP.

96    Sneden, Robert Knox. *Plan of the Battle of Honey Hill, South Carolina, November 30th.* Map. 1864.
      https://www.loc.gov/item/gvhs01.vhs00181/

100   Morand, Agustus, photographer. "[Portrait of James Beecher in military uniform]" Photograph. Brooklyn, New York, ca. 1864-1866. BSFP.

102   Gibson, James F., photographer. "[Savage Station, Virginia. Union field hospital after the battle of June 27.]" Photograph. 1862. LOC.
      https://www.loc.gov/item/2018671740/

106   Marching On!—The Fifty-Fifth Massachusetts Colored Regiment Singing John Brown's March in the Streets of Charleston, February 21, 1865. Illustration. *Harper's Weekly*, March 18, 1865, 165.

108   "[Survey photo of Zion Presbyterian Church (123 Calhoun Street).]" Photograph. Gibbes Museum of Art, 1941.

112   A Man Knows A Man. Illustration. *Harper's Weekly*, April 22, 1865, 255.

116   Knox, Thomas Wallace. *Life and Work of Henry Ward Beecher: An Authentic, Impartial and Complete History of His Public Career and Private Life from the Cradle to the Grave.* Illustration. Hartford: Hartford Publishing Company, 1887.

117   McCarthy, Eugene. *Familiar Fish: Their Habits and Capture; A Practical Book On Fresh-Water Game Fish.* Illustration. New York: D. Appleton and Company, 1900.

119(t) French, J. H, L. G Dawson, Robert Pearsall Smith, and Dawson & Co Taintor. *Map of Ulster Co., New York: from actual surveys.* Map. Philadelphia: Taintor, Dawson & Co., publishers, 1858. LOC.
      https://www.loc.gov/item/2013593238/

*119(b)*  United States Geological Survey. *Ulster County, New York.* Map. https://gis.orangecountygov.com/orange/

*121*  Van Put, Lee, photographer. "Reflection at Beecher Lake." Photograph. Livingston Manor: Lee Van Put, c2020.

*122*  Bardwell, George W. How We Fished the Wilsons. Illustration. *Outing Magazine*, September 1889, 458.

*126*  Beecher Perkins, Frances. A Seven Years' Outing. Photograph. *New England Magazine*, July 1900, 599.

*127*  Holberton, W. The Pleasures of Fly Fishing. Illustration. *Outing Magazine*, June 1889, 199.

*128*  A Postman Doing His Rounds. Illustration. *Illustrated London News*, October 30, 1880, 14.

*133*  Van Put, Ed, photographer. "Beaverkill School House." Photograph. Livingston Manor: Ed Van Put, c2015.

*134*  Kilburn Brothers, photographer. "Now we go." Photograph. New York Public Library Digital Collections. https://digitalcollections.nypl.org/items/510d47e1-7a4c-a3d9-e040-e00a18064a99

*137*  Judd, David W. Beecher's Clearing. Illustration. *American Agriculturist*, September 1881, 354.

*140*  Rhead, Louis. Brook Trout Fishing. Illustration. *Brooklyn Daily Eagle*, March 8, 1908, 21.

*142*  Judd, David W. Beecher's Clearing. Illustration. *American Agriculturist*, September 1881, 354.

*145*  Crandall, Lathan A. *Days in the Open.* Illustration. New York: Fleming H. Revell Company, 1914.

*147*  Beecher, James Chaplin. Illustration. *The National Cyclopaedia of American Biography, Vol. III.* New York: James T. White & Co., 1891.

*149*  Davis, Theo, artist. Interior of Plymouth Church—The Historical Meeting. Illustration. *Harper's Weekly*, October 19, 1872, 812.

151 Davis, Theo, artist. The Plymouth Bethel, Hicks Street. Illustration. *Harper's Weekly*, October 19, 1872, 812.

153 Seton, Ernest Thompson. *The Book of Woodcraft and Indian Lore*. Garden City, New York: Doubleday, Page & Company, 1925.

157 Myers, photographer. "[Portrait of James Beecher]" Photograph. Poughkeepsie, N.Y. ca. 1865-1880. BSFP.

160 Seely, W. T., photographer. "[Portrait of James Beecher and his wife, Frances.]" Photograph. Elmira, N.Y. ca. 1861-1866. BSFP.

# Index

## About the Author

Ed Van Put is an angling historian, author, and avid fly fisherman. He culminated a forty-year career as a fisheries professional with the New York State Department of Environmental Conservation. Ed has written extensively on fly fishing and its history in the Catskills, including several essential books. His first book *The Beaverkill: The History of a River and Its People*—released in 1996 and later expanded & revised in 2016—is the definitive book on the famous trout stream. *Trout Fishing in the Catskills* received similar acclaim as a must-read expansive exploration of the development of the Catskills as a premiere trout fishing destination. His articles have appeared in *The Conservationist*, *Trout*, *Fly Fisherman*, *Fly Rod & Reel*, and elsewhere. Ed was a founding member of the Beamoc Chapter of Trout Unlimited, as well as a founding member of the Catskill Fly Tiers Guild. He lives along the Willowemoc Creek in Livingston Manor, with his wife Judy.